"*No jargon, no grandiloquence, nice humor.*"
—Nuala Gallagher, Communications and Marketing Specialist

"*The book does a wonderful job of drawing in a diversity of scoops, stories, and tips. It covers lots in an engaging fashion.*"
—Frédéric Dubois, Journalist & Documentary maker

"*This is sure to be an important read. Journalism can often seem like a black box to the uninitiated, making it harder to discern with accuracy the stories you can trust from those you oughtn't. There's a rigour below the surface of good journalism that can go unrewarded in the world of clickbait and [words stick in craw] 'fake news.*"
—Alex Webb, Columnist Bloomberg Opinion

BEHIND THE SCOOP

Why You Should Think & Act Like a Journalist

JOHANNES KOCH

BEHIND THE SCOOP

ISBN: 9798590345298

Visit www.jarkoch.com for more information about the author.

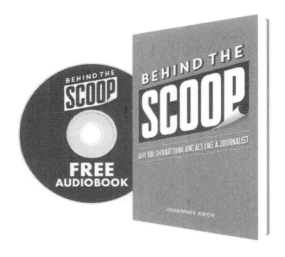

DOWNLOAD THE AUDIOBOOK FOR FREE!

Just to say thanks for buying my book, I'd like to give you the audiobook version for free.

Go here to download:

https://bit.ly/FreeBTSAudiobook

CONTENTS

PART I:
What makes an excellent journalist
(and how you can think like one)

PART II:
What makes a scoop
(and how to write one)

PART III:
A journalist's manifesto
(and why we need more journalists)

BONUS

INTRODUCTION

"I think this profession is what God wants me to do. It's my fate." — Amindeh Blaise Atabong, Investigative Journalist

Journalists want scoops.

What is a scoop? Why do journalists want them? Are all journalists gunning for prizes and recognition, chasing scoops left and right? If you want a scoop too, how on earth would you get one?

In financial journalism, scoops are defined as stories that move a share price. In financial newsroom parlance, these scoops move the needle. Like a Geiger counter, these stories rattle the share prices in a way that gets you a measurable response. That's one form of impact that journalism can have.

Journalists want impact.

Investors care a great deal about the companies that make up the stock markets of the world. Their livelihoods depend on buying low and selling high to make money. A writer, meanwhile, likes to see the effect of their published story. Share price up, or share price down—either way, it doesn't matter but the journalist knows their part in making it move.

Elsewhere in journalism, impact is fairly straightforward: it means the occasional call from a happy or angry reader. It's the number of clicks or views on a story. By those metrics, a journalist knows they've been heard, but they still wonder: *Did I say something meaningful and was I taken seriously? How am I supposed to know if I am making a difference?*

1

Journalists want to make a difference.

You don't become a journalist to make millions. You become a journalist driven by a sense of purpose—which you may sense as a God-given purpose or maybe just the desire to see a better world. But sometimes there are gaps between your ideals and the reality of your day job.

For me it was exhilarating to see a share price soar or tank as a result of my journalism. With two massive screens and a myriad of blinking lights and alarm bells at my side, I could react to every hiccup that affected the companies I covered at *Bloomberg*, the global financial information powerhouse.

The *Bloomberg* newsroom in Berlin was a mix of murmurs punctuated by the occasional bursts of activity as breaking news crashed in. Editors shouted "backread" or "can someone come look over my shoulder" as news was prepped at lightning speed for release on the wire. With an event like Brexit, the red oozed down my black screen as markets shuddered and the financial world felt on the verge of total collapse and chaos.

I came to journalism over a decade ago, initially with visions of being a writer at a newspaper, holed up in a quiet room after returning from assignment on some far-flung island. Upon my entry to the profession, however, newspapers were dying out like swing parties in the Great Depression. Online news was the new swing dance of my 20s and I liked a good party, so that's the one I joined. I ended up in financial journalism in London first, where functional, precise and factual writing eradicated the need for stories told with flair. That made me less of a journalist, I thought.

But I am a journalist, just one that was created during a financial crisis, came of age on a clunky content management system, and never put in the hard yards at a newspaper writing about guinea pig races. As an aspiring writer, my hopes and dreams of becoming a "real" journalist seemed dashed, but journalism is about more than writing.

My original sense of purpose as a journalist was simply to "make the world a better place." At first, it didn't seem I was accomplishing that within financial reporting. Most people don't care if a stock price moves. Why would they? Beyond a financial crisis or unless they own or trade the stock, it doesn't affect them.

It took me a long time to realize that there are at least two major types of journalists: those who report and gather intelligence for special interest groups, and those who report for a wider public.

Writing for the elite, as I still do as a freelance reporter for investor publications, is an opportunity to influence and garner respect. My work reaches into the echelons of power. This journalism doesn't help the wider public make better decisions about their lives. Neither is better or worse, they just serve different purposes.

Journalism is inherently activist, whether it's behind a paywall or not. I knew I was building skills in financial journalism. Ensuring investors have the best, the latest, and most accurate information turns on and off the money tap. I was, and still am, acting on their behalf. I also still believed those same skills could be leveraged to build a more equitable world.

The skills required in this career—to unearth market-moving stories, get behind a secretive deal or pinpoint the figures a company is trying to obscure—are valuable, but they're not the only way in which I think and act like a journalist. Being a journalist is an ethos that anyone can adopt to become more critical, creative and courageous and that's at the heart of this book.

You don't become a journalist to be happy. You become one because you're unhappy with the world as it is and you want to see change. That's at the core of journalism and why thinking and acting like a journalist is so powerful.

Journalism and its little cousin 'the news business' (or what we might call commoditized news) is in the middle of a gargantuan transformation not seen since the advent of the printing press. The skill and craft of the 20th-century breed of journalist is disappearing at a time when those sorts of reporters are needed more than ever.

In case your local newspaper or source still exists, it collects, organizes, verifies, and explains important events but it's not your primary information source anymore. People get information in an uncurated form online, either combing the Internet for the information they want or receiving it passively according to algorithms that don't inherently serve humanity's interests.

As the global COVID-19 pandemic has shown, the way information flows through the systems of search and social media requires that everyone think and act a little bit more like a journalist. We should ask: *What is true, does this matter to me, should I care?* Sorting fact from fiction is now, more than ever, an individual responsibility as the pace and density of casual information drowns out serious reporting and journalism.

Like travel agents (also a profession in peril), journalists still have their place. Journalists are always asking, "Why does this matter?" Journalists are hunting for the truth in an attempt to make sense of the world by asking questions, probing and being critical of what they are being fed.

The average news consumer is not actually in control of the news they consume. They think they're choosing freely but an algorithm has already suggested the destination. They are not trained in fact-checking, critically appraising sources, or sorting out what could matter to them as voters, students, neighbors, parents, or otherwise. They are not paid to do it, so they cannot spend much time doing it. They aren't accountable for their results, and they don't benefit from their colleagues' oversight.

This is not to say journalists' work is perfect but there is a useful mindset in our approach to sorting through the intricately spun web of information. We uncover secrets because we look closely at the statements, the documents, and the numbers. We develop professional expertise, and for the lucky ones, we are compensated for it.

News organizations once acted as an interface between democratic institutions and the public at large, facilitating the democratic process. Even if they are politically biased, you know what you hold in your hands. Now, that responsibility has been devolved to each person as an individual to discern fact from fiction. We are now tasked with acting as our own gateways in the information process with a power to distribute that information to those who "follow" us online (whether they number one or one million).

Liberal democracies thrive on small, meaningful, individual action. Greta Thunberg's action on the climate crisis, in other words, or that of individuals who hold power to account on particular local or global issues. Democracies, for all their imperfections, seem to have endured and to be worth fighting for. I live in one, and I still believe in its power to protect individual rights, freedom of speech and the right to participate in elections and select our leaders. I'm not ready to give up on it. Are you?

This book is a search for what makes great journalism and its benefits to democracy. In the process, it attempts to define an ethos to help anyone think and act like a journalist to stem the tide of misinformation and fake news, and to elevate individual responsibility.

I've come to love my work as a journalist because even when I'm not publishing information for my readers, my words and actions help those around me navigate the information-chaos by asking questions, probing our own beliefs, and searching for answers and demanding truth and transparency.

Journalistic rigor grew out of the necessity to manage information flows, so there is a lot to be learned by approaching your news consumption in this way. The lessons we've learned are a template for anyone trying to get a little closer to the truth. (If journalists are a dying breed, it is that much more important to preserve these skills.)

Before we get started, here's an overview on what you'll find in this book.

WHAT'S IN THIS BOOK

You're here to find out how journalists operate. This book illuminates the importance of journalistic work and justifies why we do things the way we do them.

You'll see how journalists deal with sources and other insights about their work that you can't find in other books or manuals. All these insights are important to recognize good journalism, bad practice, and help anyone who's fed up with reading the news to pick a piece of journalism that's worth their time.

This book is not a writing manual. If you want to learn about journalistic writing there are plenty of resources. This book supplements other writing and craft books with the inspirational secret-sauce, attitudes and knowledge to understand scoops.

You'll come away understanding how scoops are generated, how to spot a good story and why journalists pick a particular lead. You'll understand how stories are pieced together and what parts are needed to make them work, without getting technical about how they're written.

The final part of this book is a manifesto on why we need less news and more journalists. It is an appeal for everyone to think and act more like a journalist in today's digital, information-first environment.

This journalistic culture and approach must not be lost in the world of on-demand personal information. If we all adopted a few of the characteristics that make journalists outstanding at navigating fake news, including conscious information gathering and carefully considered word-choice, and if we all sought the truth while bravely admitting mistakes, we would be better off.

This book is not a work of academic analyses with sample sizes, key findings, and conclusions. It's a guide, a loose tapestry of views to help anyone who wants to get a sense of what happens behind the scoop, understand the potential of journalism, anticipate the challenges journalists face, and acquire some insight.

Beyond that, it's a book to champion the tough work journalists do, inspire young journalists, and help anyone improve their understanding of a journalist's work from a practitioner's perspective. I'm unvarnished and biased in saying that this book celebrates journalists' work, which brings me to the scoopsters who made this book come alive.

THE SCOOPSTERS

The most important ingredient of this book and the reason it exists is thanks to the journalists I interviewed and the stories we discussed. Each journalist provided a shred of information and a unique perspective that informed and shaped the ideas found in these pages.

They get our full attention here for a brief moment before appearing throughout this book.

I introduce each journalist so you can get a sense of their caliber and an overview of the articles we discussed. I refer to these stories liberally throughout. To keep track of their names—empathizing with you, it's a lot to keep track of!—I've put these summaries here, in one place, as a reference for you.

Abhijeet Gurjar is a freelance photojournalist based in Kolhapur, Maharashtra, India, whose work has been syndicated by Reuters and all major national Indian newspapers. I spoke to him about disaster coverage and the severe flooding of his region in the monsoon of 2019. He went on a mission to document a rescue operation that went awry and then ended up covering how the rescue team had to be rescued in treacherous conditions. During the last major flood, a boat had capsized and many lives were lost. These pictures were published in *The Hindu* and *U.S. News & World Report*, *CNBC* and the *Gulf Times*.

Amindeh Blaise Atabong is a freelance journalist based in Yaoundé, Cameroon. He's the journalist behind the story "Inside 'Ambazonia,'" a lengthy investigation into the impact of a heart-wrenching and long-drawn-out conflict rooted in Cameroon's bilingual colonial history. He shed light on a dogged civil war with a high death toll as extremists looking to create Ambazonia, a country for Cameroon's Anglophones who feel discriminated against, clashed with its French-led government compatriots. His fearless coverage put him at the heart of the conflict, where he spoke to residents and explained both the conflict and its consequences. "Inside 'Ambazonia'" was a finalist in the 2019 True Story Awards, and Atabong has been awarded the Kurt Schork Memorial Award in International Journalism.

Arlis Alikaj is an Albanian freelance investigative journalist who came to journalism as an urban planner with a degree in geoinformation engineering. His story "Chainsaw Gangs: The Plunder of Albania's Ancient Forests" is an investigative piece that exposes illegal logging in Albania's national park Shebenik-Jabllanicë, a UNESCO world heritage site. The story was funded by the Balkan Investigative Reporting Network and published regionally in eight languages. He has been a freelance journalist locally and nationally but this was his breakout piece. The story's impact was far-reaching regionally: it helped put an end to the illegal logging and sounded the alarm bells on corruption in Albania.

Anna Codrea-Rado is a British-born freelance journalist who has written for every imaginable outlet including, but not limited to, *The New York Times*, *The Guardian*, *VICE*, *The Paris Review*, *New York Magazine*, *WIRED*, *Quartz*, *The Atlantic*, and the *BBC*. She writes about culture and technology and sends out a newsletter called *The Professional Freelancer* on making a career out of freelance journalism.

The Guardian story "'I'm a rabbit girl': the woman accused of hoarding bunnies in Brooklyn" is a profile on a woman vilified as a bunny hoarder and facing jail time for what she sees as rescuing animals.

Bobby Ross Jr. is the editor-in-chief of *The Christian Chronicle*, an international newspaper for Churches of Christ with 138,000 print subscribers in the US. He's a classically trained reporter with over three decades of experience in covering religion, having produced thousands of stories. We discuss "A Perpetrator in the Pews," which kicks off with a judge's decision on a sex offender which feeds into a more in-depth investigation into a sex offender who continues to trouble the congregation. The scoop exposes double standards and nepotism in church leadership.

Daniel Bates is an award-winning multimedia journalist based out of New York with several decades of experience reporting for *The Guardian, The Daily Beast, The International Business Times, The Times,* and *The Daily Mail.* As a correspondent for *The Daily Mail,* he has been covering longer and more arduous stories such as the one into late financier and pedophile Jeffrey Epstein. We look at his investigation "Revealed: Flight logs prove Duke of York's Epstein girl WAS at key locations and on each occasion, Prince Andrew was never far away—so now will he help her lawyers?" The story is one among his many investigations to uncover how several important people aided, or were indirectly complicit in, Epstein's sex trafficking.

Jop de Vrieze is a Dutch freelance science journalist with a background in biomedical sciences. The story we discussed for this book won him and his wife, Zvezdana Vukojevic, the AAAS Kavli Science Journalism Award. "It is a beautiful child, why did he die?" tells the story of their own still-born child and uncovers a kink in the Dutch natal care system's armour, which relies heavily on midwives to deliver care. De

Vrieze shows how midwives are a weak link in the healthcare system and financially incentivized to keep women in their care amid heavily disputed risk selection signals to prevent stillbirths.

Lewis Raven Wallace is an independent transgender journalist in North Carolina who's a regular contributor to and former political editor at *Scalawag*, a publication for southern US states and communities. His work has appeared in the *Columbia Journalism Review* and *Nieman Reports*, with his audio work in places such as *NPR*. We discuss his *Scalawag* story "In a small Georgia city, an unpaid court fine can get your utilities cut off" which investigates a racially-charged policy that disproportionately affects blacks and the poor. In LaGrange, unpaid fines for small violations were being tacked on utility bills with threats of losing water or electricity if they remained unpaid. In his book *The View from Somewhere: Undoing the Myth of Journalistic Objectivity,* he looks at the history of "objectivity" in journalism and why we may need to dispense with it.

Oliver Staley is based out of New York and is an editor at *Quartz*. Before taking over as editor of the culture and lifestyle section, he covered everything from entertainment, fashion, travel, education and healthcare. We look at his story, "The future of stroke patients may depend on the part-time job of a Canadian surgeon." It is as much a profile of one man seeking a cure for stroke—where the pharmaceutical industry has failed to find adequate treatments—as about the inequalities that dictate the market. The protagonist has a huge task, not only from a scientific perspective, but from a social one: people in lower-income countries suffer from less access to newly developed drugs.

Sarah Syed is a technology reporter at *Bloomberg*. Before that and during the research for this book, she was a private equity correspondent at the newswire covering deals, mergers and acquisitions. Her story "Colgate is said to join bidding for Nestlé skin-health business" is a market-moving-style scooplet (more on that term later) in a series of reports that looked at the sale of Nestlé's skincare business. The story required several reporters to collaborate to get investors the latest intel on the deal. The business was eventually sold to a consortium of investors for $10.2 billion. In this high-stakes story, Syed and her colleagues uncovered that Colgate might throw the hungry financial investors off balance with a bid.

Shalini Singh is an independent journalist, formerly a principal correspondent for the *Hindustan Times* and *The Week* in Delhi, India. She won India's highest award for environmental journalism in 2013 and produced the scoop "Is India's sunshine state gouging itself out?" Her story on illegal mining in India's smallest state shows how the pursuit of iron-ore and profits has had disastrous social and ecological consequences as the government turns a blind eye. She continues to report on the cross-section between the environment and society.

Veronica Zaragovia is a Colombian-born radio, print, video and photojournalist who has reported across the globe from the US to Hong Kong for *NPR*, *Al Jazeera English*, *Time Out*, *Fodor's Travel*, the *Associated Press*, *Time*, and the *BBC*. We looked at a story she did in Colombia: "From cocaine to cacao: one man's mission to save Colombia's farmers through chocolate." It takes the reader into the heart of Colombia's rural communities with a positive slant on an entrepreneur's efforts to persuade Afro-Colombians to plant cocoa.

You'll find out more about the journalists featured in this book, including their audio recordings, pictures, links to social accounts, and copies of their articles and photos in the book vault (johannes-koch-freelance.ck.page/91de9125e2). These stories are all snapshots of their time, and in time, all scoops become dated. What was news is only news until someone reads it, then it is history (as the saying goes).

Zaragovia's story doesn't conclude; governments change, and programs to help farmers make the switch take time. By contrast, Syed's story on Nestlé's skin-health business came to a conclusion with a consortium of investors. It would be a waste of time and space to follow each story in this way.

These articles stand as a record of their time and, for the purpose of examination, their eventual conclusions are not material to this book. If you're interested in Jeffrey Epstein or mining in India, there's a world of research waiting out there for you. Instead I focus on how these journalists found their scoops.

I didn't want to frontload this book with a diatribe on my research process so have tagged a section to the end of this book which dives into that, if you are interested. There is also some bonus material at the end to say thanks for sticking around and reading these pages.

Needless to say that all of the journalists I interviewed for this book are spirited, lively, and brilliant. Their views are supplemented by those of other excellent journalists collected from books, articles, and podcasts.

What makes an excellent journalist? That's the subject of Part I, which is where this book continues. If you're more interested in what makes an excellent story, jump to Part II; for why you should think and act like a journalist, proceed to Part III.

PART I

What makes an excellent journalist
(and how you can think like one)

Facts, Truth & Reach

"Truth is found at the bottom of a bottomless pit." —Jonathan Harr, *A Civil Action*

The earth orbits the sun. In astronomy, that's an objective truth. Science holds many objective truths. Take gravity.

Gravity is neither good nor bad, it's an objective truth. Planes need to conquer it to get off the ground, but otherwise humans celebrate it as without it we'd be floating around haplessly.

It can be perceived as good or bad, depending on the perspective.

When I try to philosophize on the idea of truth, I keep coming back to one extreme realist: Epimenides of Knossos, himself a Cretan, who made the paradoxical statement that all Cretans are liars.

In human thought there is not one truth but many truths. They are, in essence, interpretations or arrangements of facts to suit either political or personal needs.

Not every claim is defensible. Holocaust deniers and climate deniers are simply wrong—in many cases, intentionally and maliciously so. The factual evidence that the genocide took place and that climate is changing is overwhelming, which does not permit us to debate the basics. In other areas, though, facts can be assembled in different ways to create different versions of truth.

Understanding those varying perspectives and how these versions are assembled based on factual evidence is, in essence, the hallmark of great journalism. It will help the reader find their own truth as even in the greatest of disagreements there are shared facts but also personal truths.

Good journalism is based on a journalist's thoughtful decisions, and the assembly of those decisions sometimes leads to a version of the truth that we, as journalists, are looking for. Journalists strive to be the best conduit of a truth, although they don't always achieve that.

The scoops I've outlined in this book are testament to the idea that there are versions of many truths, and different versions may be defensible as long as they are based on facts. Facts give rise to a shared reality and the factual experiences should be similar. Consensus needs to be built around facts: either gravity exists or it doesn't. How we then decide to interpret that fact in the context of the story is based on a unique perspective.

Even in the hardest-hitting story on social exclusion, discrimination or abuse, where the facts are agreed upon and the general ethical problem is obvious, the deeper meaning will be felt differently by individuals and communities. The question will always remain: What does this mean for me and for my community? What is "my truth" that I take away from this story?

ALTERNATE REALITIES

I got off a phone call one day, absorbing the shocking reality that some people don't believe what's in the news. "It's all fake news. The media has been coerced and manipulated to mislead the public," a close friend told me over the line.

I'm sure he remembered he was talking not just to a friend but to a journalist. I couldn't let that stand but, in good faith, I kept an open mind about why he might think this. We talked.

My friend said he didn't know what to believe anymore and would much rather get his information from alternative sources and media. *What alternative sources do you consult?* I didn't really get an immediate answer but I did get links to Telegram threads and YouTubers.

Why isn't that information fake news? Why does he trust those sources over, say, something like *The New York Times* or the *BBC*?

He told me about the views he held and where he got them from. Some of them were clearly not mainstream, which is fine, but they seemed wonkish, often wrapped in smart assertions devoid of fact with an unhealthy serving of conjecture. It was enjoyable to listen to these ideas initially but I then also spent a considerable amount of time looking into some of the theories to find that they weren't fact-based.

If you believe that the powers of global institutions overreach and are a threat to sovereignty, you might, as a consequence, buy into several more ideas. Take this one: media organisations are often owned by wealthy individuals for profit, and these organisations have agendas. Is that true? Sometimes yes, sometimes no.

Jeff Bezos, the billionaire CEO of Amazon, also owns *The Washington Post*. *The Guardian*, by contrast, is a reader-funded organisation held by a trust. Which outlet has more of an "agenda?" *The Guardian* has taken a stand on climate change and uses the "climate crisis" in its reporting which is a much stronger term. Is *The Guardian* more or less trustworthy on this point just because it is run by a trust and not by a billionaire?

In another example, one such "alternative" source my skeptical friend suggested held that the World Health Organization (WHO) has direct authority to lock down countries in the event of a pandemic. Of course, it does not. It has no such authority over nations, nor does it have an army.

Nations do, however, make laws based on the WHO's recommendations, which are themselves the result of a global coordinated scientific effort. Are these recommendations tainted by political bias and the disproportionate funding structures of the WHO? Yes.

Are the people that run these organizations often from the very industries they are supposed to curtail? Yes.

Does the WHO have the power to set a nation's policy? Indirectly, yes.

But does the owner of a media organisation—who is, after all, just one individual, no matter how wealthy—have the power to control multiple, amorphous forces in a globally interdependent world? Unlikely.

"Unlikely" sows doubt, which allows new ideas to enter and germinate. While doubt can stimulate research, it's also common for a skeptical attitude to be handled less carefully and for the skeptical person to yield to false beliefs. I've known this but it was reinforced in a big way during the exchange with my friend.

I didn't expect to change his view; I just shared some facts to dispel a false assertion. His belief probably wouldn't change. Nevertheless, I had to try. A cornerstone of being a journalist is to take at face value someone's assertion, do your homework, go down the rabbit hole and then emerge with an answer based on factual evidence.

Being critical of global institutions is a valid view. There is ample evidence to support their ineffectiveness. There's a great debate to be had and we should have that debate.

But being critical of "the mainstream media" is dangerous. "The media" are our sources of information, and "the mainstream" ones are generally those that have stood the test of time or that have the best funding and institutional support. Once you've accepted the premise that all information is "fake news," you've thrown out a system that includes important journalistic work as a whole.

You'll latch on to whatever belief you hold, no matter how extreme. Let's call it the QAnon phenomenon, in which politicians invoke the QAnon conspiracy to get elected. In this case the right-wing conspiracy claims that a cabal of satanic pedophiles is co-opting the institutions of government. (There is no evidence for this. Any "evidence" makes sense only within the internal world of the conspiracy theory. Also note that conspiracies exist on both sides of the political aisle: take the left-wing conspiracy theory that 9/11 was an inside job.)

Conspiracy theories confirm a person's already entrenched belief. But if we throw out the baby with the bathwater, at the very least we need to become aware that we are doing so.

We need to become aware of the echo chamber on Facebook, where all our friends, with similar backgrounds and points of view, share the same ideas, opinions and perspectives. We need to be aware that our views are being limited by the input we allow in and reflect upon.

It seems harmless but when we reach into other communal spheres we keep these confirmation bias-blinders on. Like horses we pull a carriage of different beliefs along the road and can't see anything but our road ahead, regardless of whether there's a broken bridge ahead with people on the sidelines urging us to slow down before it's too late.

CONFIRMATION BIAS

"If you consume a lot of news pieces you can have the craziest theory about the world in your mind and you will always find news pieces that will confirm your crazy idea about the world and, that's the danger." — Anna Codrea-Rado, Journalist

The Swiss essayist Rolf Dobelli used the following example to demonstrate confirmation bias and what we need to do about it. Let's run a little experiment and have some fun.

I'm going to give you a sequence of numbers. You need to guess what you think the next number in the sequence will be (oh, and don't jump ahead or you'll ruin the fun).

Ready? Here's the sequence:

2, 4, 6, 8, 10...

Okay. Got it? What's the next number? Got it? Hold it in your mind.

Now, what is the rule these numbers follow? Say that rule out loud (or in your head, if you like).

You're thinking 12 and your rule is even numbers. Right? But if I told you 13 was right, and so was 18, and 21, would you be confused?

(Dobelli really got us here.)

Your theory implied that the next number is 12. That's a valid guess, but my rule is simply that the numbers keep increasing. That is the rule, and it just so happened the preceding numbers were evenly spread.

To get to the truth, you would have to undermine your favourite theory. (In this case, even numbers.) You need to seek out disconfirming evidence. If you could have asked me first, you could have thrown out a few numbers and, as long as they were bigger, you would have disconfirmed your first theory and had the opportunity to form a better theory.

"You have to actively fight that tendency to find those numbers that fit your theory. You have to actively try to disconfirm the evidence at hand to figure out what the theory is," as Dobelli says.

This is exactly what journalists do on a day-to-day basis when we check facts, ask for replies from all the parties in our story and consider each piece of information we choose to share. We are looking for as many avenues and ways to disconfirm the information before us and to come up with better theories that are supported by the evidence, thus strengthening the stories we'll publish.

Shoestring reporting is essentially that: You pull at each factual thread in the story and try to confirm it in multiple ways.

Which is why the encounter with my friend on the subject of the WHO was so frustrating. He presented his view as a fact, yet he lacked evidence to back it up. He was taking the words of so-called alternative media to confirm a strongly held belief that global institutions are corrupt, mismanaged and dangerous. This "alternative media" doesn't necessarily take into account reporting rigour, fairness and the high demands of accuracy.

Confirmation bias is also why Facebook and other web algorithms are so potent. They continue to assess, surmise and characterize what you have already consumed, locking you into that echo chamber.

Assumptions will continue to confirm a trend or prevailing bias based on what you've read or clicked—for example, liberal news or conservative news—and then this bias is exploited. Internet companies build a picture of who you are and then exploit that narrative, sometimes to the extreme. Leaving those echo chambers on a regular basis is crucial.

What my friend did was seek out a conflicting view, which, in itself, was great. We should actively seek out perspectives that undermine our view of the world, expecting that an idea or theory might hold up or crumble. Considering the source of the old view is critical. But we must evaluate the source of the new view, too. Just because it is new and criticizes the status quo does not mean it is accurate. If we absorb news that isn't fact-based, we're susceptible to propaganda.

Journalists tend to remain open to the possibility that they are wrong. Being a truth-seeker, then, is as much about questioning reality as it is about accepting facts.

"The search for truth is what makes a good story. I'm not so presumptuous to think that I'll necessarily find it at the end of the day, but I do hope that my writing prods readers to join that search, to think about themselves and the world just a little bit differently." — Alex Kotlowitz, *The New New Journalism*

IMPACT & REACH

In the introduction, I said that journalists want to have an impact. Impact is often measured in numbers: the number of "story hits" online, and the newspaper or magazine circulation in print.

How many people have read the story? How many people have shared it? The wider the reach, the more impact the article has, right? The more people read our stuff, the greater our influence as journalists. *If I splatter the Internet with enough material,* I think, *maybe I'll get noticed.*

But numbers won't tell the whole story, and "reach" doesn't always equal influence. Nobody except journalists (pretty much) looks at the byline, so even if your story gets a lot of hits, that doesn't mean readers are beginning to recognize your name.

What marketeers call "reach" isn't everything. A story's impact can be personal. "Reaching" readers in a meaningful way (not always measured in clicks and eyeballs) is at the heart of a journalist's purpose and motivation.

One basic idea behind *Bloomberg*, when I was hired there, was to reach the 100 most influential people in the world. Influence buys power, or so the thought goes. The higher the information quality, the better decisions its readers can make to maintain their wealth and get wealthier. A narrow focus like this creates a lot of impact for people with the resources to pay for it.

Bloomberg is a rare and exceptional case because its financial terminals fund one of the most expansive and well-staffed newsrooms, while non-financial news outlets are unlikely to afford the same resources.

Impact is measurable not only in reach (which is quantifiable) but in reputation and influence (which isn't). Winning a Pulitzer Prize is one highly visible result of reputation. Yet Pulitzer-winning stories have high-stakes influence of a type that isn't widely understood. Consider *Bloomberg's* 2015 Pulitzer Prize for explanatory reporting on US corporation tax dodging. This series of articles flew under the radar of the ordinary citizen but was high-impact.

A more clearly measurable metric in this high-octane financial news environment is the movement of a company's share price. Granted, a company's own announcements can lead to a dramatic rise and fall of its share price, but sometimes journalists scoop those announcements or unveil other corporate corruption or malfeasance to move the stock. The journalists and *Bloomberg* terminal readers gain a competitive advantage from knowing that first.

This type of information directly impacts reader's decisions. The possibility of profit greases the cost-benefit analysis of paying for the *Bloomberg* terminal. One shred of the right information in a sea of financial data will easily cover the costs of "the terminal," the name for its financial information portal. Inevitably, many traders—regardless of whether they read *Bloomberg*—will lose money, but that's the nature of the game.

And more often than not, reach is coveted more than quality, especially online where "reach" is quantifiable as more clicks and advertising revenue and better search rankings, leading to more traffic and, once more, advertising revenue.

But, of course, quality matters, too. To many journalists, each story feels big and important, as we hope our work reaches the person who just needs to hear it or helps them discover something new and valuable to them.

Scoops often build over time. Many are boring and don't garner widespread attention on first glance. So "reach" alone can't judge a scoop. Scoops already fit a purpose beyond plain news which Rob Wijnberg, founding editor of *The Correspondent*, appropriately described as "sensational, exceptional, current events."

Metrics won't drive investigations of the type done by the journalists I interviewed for this book. There isn't always an immediate need for "public service" journalism. Reporting on the Watergate scandal (with the result of journalists holding power to account and doing their job) was largely imperceptible and built over several months and weeks. There's not one Watergate story that lands a knock-out punch, but the impact of that overall story was broad and visceral.

Impact will depend on what you ascribe to a story beyond just the numbers. In fact, journalists often choose to measure it in their own way.

As a student journalist Atabong sought to cover the celebrations of Cameroonian separatists, who claimed southern Cameroon as an independent state. His presence was met with hostility as the illegal celebrations were broken up by police. Camera in hand, he was slapped in the face, arrested and detained for the day as one of the separatists. The impact of covering the story and the experience was profound, emboldening Atabong to pursue his work as a journalist professionally.

He said: "I felt more confident because I thought I was one of the luckiest journalists that was locked up just for a day. Other journalists have been jailed, exiled. So that did not stop me."

In my work as a financial journalist, I often found the impact I had on the world at large was limited. I was gathering information on companies, markets and people that made for poor dinner party conversation.

I found strength in the impact I was having as a journalist and in the privilege I had of speaking to company spokespeople. I attributed my impact to the integrity with which I approached my work. I'd pride myself on trying to be as professional as possible in my conduct, because I knew that people would walk away from an interaction with me feeling like it was time well-spent and that I had taken their views into consideration. I was annoyed on behalf of people who felt used by journalists in their previous interactions.

Integrity earned me at least some trust among sources who were then willing to talk to me despite strict non-disclosure agreements or other impediments. There was real-world impact of my stories (I've moved some company stock prices), so people who work for those companies might be understandably nervous about sharing information with me, but in dealing with people one-on-one I made sure those interactions were impactful on a personal level so I left a lasting, professional and cordial impression. The visible success of these interactions has made my work worthwhile.

Journalists are uniquely positioned because we're not trying to sell anything (okay, I am selling my book *Break into Journalism: Contact-Building Tools & Tactics*, which talks about this). While some people feel compromised, co-opted, or used by certain journalists, this need not be the outcome. The journalist is free simply to tell someone's story, and that might be the type of interaction that restores dignity to someone's battered existence or takes them down, depending on how the journalist treats them during the interview and within the published story.

There is something especially civil about being a journalist and that civility is sometimes carried into the world as we care for it by telling people's stories. At heart, we are people who want to change the world and spread civility. Codrea-Rado balances the one-sided, often discriminatory or predatory reporting that preceded her piece; in hers, she attempts to restore some dignity to the protagonist without ignoring the facts.

Headlines regularly referred to Dorota Trec, the main character, as a bunny or rabbit hoarder but never took a more nuanced approach to include her perspective, preferring instead to focus on the sensationalism of her conviction and labelling the woman as a hoarder. This is a label she may not be deserving of.

Not everything is black and white, nor is it always easy to describe a shade of grey. Sometimes the journalist needs to acknowledge different possible interpretations and allow the reader to choose where to place their sympathy.

Three years later, Codrea-Rado's article is still at the top of Google's search rankings for "bunny hoarder" with the title that starts with a quote from Trec: "I'm a rabbit girl." The impact of the story might be seen in redressing the balance and providing a much-needed and nuanced perspective.

Scoops are scoops by virtue of serving some greater purpose beyond just plain news. A reader may change their mind or experience a paradigm shift after reading it. The scoop might inform a debate, force a comment from someone in power, charge a community with ammunition for their cause and fuel policy change that has real-world consequences for its citizens. At its best, which is also its rarest form, a scoop exposes corruption and challenges power, and this will have far-reaching financial, political and social implications.

- The ministry that ignored Alikaj's calls for comment finally contacted him after the story went public. He pressed hard for a comment prior to publication but was met with resistance. The story had both a local and regional impact and was picked up by a regional environmental forum taking place around that time, giving the activists and NGOs proof to hold up. This allowed activists to inform public policy. The story may also have emboldened citizen protests. All this forced an emergency moratorium which blocked the timber industry, so his undercover work in the forest had far-reaching implications.

- Gurjar's foray into the wild to get a snap of the rescue operation challenged the official storyline that better flood defenses had been put in place. Though more severe tragedies had befallen the region in the decade before his reporting, the shot helped illuminate ineffective management of flood disaster relief and response in the region. It continued to inform the debate to improve disaster mechanisms.

- Bates's scoops on Prince Andrew within the Epstein saga continued to keep the pressure on a public figure who had information about the disgraced financier.

- De Vrieze's story on his stillborn child got him invited to parliamentary debates to answer questions based on what the story unveiled. The story also angered a community of midwives, whose proponents spent time and energy trying to discredit de Vrieze, which in turn forced more heated and lively political debate. De Vrieze received accolades and remained sanguine about the lasting impact he may have had. "Did it have a lasting effect? I'm not sure. Of course there's a lot of things going on, but at least everybody is still remembering that, okay, what we're talking about is saving babies. And I think that we did make a difference," he said. The Dutch healthcare system continues to reform prenatal care to this day.

It might not be important how many people a journalist reaches but it is essential to reach the right people. Ross's story was destined for the Churches of Christ communities served by the newspaper *The Christian Chronicle*, so it was the people in those communities who mattered to him. Though I learn a thing or two by reading the story, I'm disconnected from the events. I can only feel outrage and shock, but the story was praised by the community who thanked him for exposing this dark material. More victims came forward, and there was a stronger community drive to stop pedophilia and sexual abuse in the churches.

If anything, as Ross said, these cases can't just be swept under the carpet. They need to be dealt with.

Impact is imperceptible in many instances. It remains invisible because we can't see into our readers' heads to know whether we have changed their minds about something, riled them up or given them a new platform to make just the right decision at the right juncture. Sometimes, journalists doubt themselves, and wonder: Why bother at all?

Egos, Mistakes & Liars

It is never wise for a journalist to "become the news." Most journalists want to shine a light on their subjects, not on themselves, and there are reasons for that. It's not because we're humble. A good story might thrust the journalist into the limelight as an expert in a subject or issue, but that's not usually the goal.

Depending on the platform, political journalists refrain from showing political bias publicly and in doing so try to report about politics as fairly as possible, even though they lean left or right on the political spectrum.

Related to this, another classic editorial guideline is that journalists shouldn't participate in open debates and forums or take sides. This might require that a journalist cover a demonstration but not march with the demonstrators, for example.

Then there's the profit motive. As a financial journalist, I don't own the stock in the companies I cover, or there would be a conflict of interest. I'm sometimes privy to market sensitive information, in which case I'd better not have stock in the company or I might be seen doing insider trading, where I share the information for my own or another person's financial gain. It's not worth going to jail over something like that.

These are all sensible precautions to keep journalists out of the news. When a well-known journalist does "become the story," it usually highlights poor conduct. Since misbehaving journalists are rare, when it does happen (or when there is an allegation of misconduct), it sticks out and makes headlines.

One tale involved *CNN*'s White House correspondent, Jim Acosta, who during one of President Donald Trump's rare press conferences apparently hogged the mic for a little too long, preventing a female aide from taking it away and passing it on to the next journalist. It cost him his White House press credentials. Never mind that President Trump had an axe to grind with *CNN* or that Acosta may have simply been seeking an answer to a question—an answer he didn't receive, after all.

The President justified taking the credentials away because the White House should "never tolerate a reporter placing his hands on a young woman just trying to do her job as a White House intern." A statement laced with spin and deception, of course, but it kept *CNN* out of the White House temporarily and made a mockery of the journalist. His credentials were eventually restored by court order, but the airtime was devoted to the Acosta mic-grab. A discussion over social media erupted over whether it was a grab, small nudge or a full-on anti-feminist assault. From a classic editorial perspective, the incident should have been avoided; the eyes should have been on the White House and its policies, not some sideshow about a journalist's conduct.

This episode goes to show that "being the story" is an ugly sideshow and journalists shouldn't let it happen. Mostly, journalists keep a low profile, stay professional, and are civil, and sometimes the best answers come to those who bide their time, rather than going on the offensive. Acosta, in demanding answers to simple questions from people in power who should be held accountable, hadn't really done much wrong.

Journalists now routinely become part of the story as it lives and breathes with the Internet. Online stories orbit around their lives.

Especially given that journalists are more intimately involved with their stories, they may see the need to keep the story updated. A deep and thorough story about an issue has a longer life on the web because it can be discovered time and time again (unlike in print) so it becomes important to update the story, often using feedback from readers, to help it maintain its relevance. This journalism is more bottom-up as it harnesses the crowd and continues to morph as time goes on.

Glen Greenwald, an attorney-cum-journalist best known for his coverage of surveillance programs based on the Edward Snowden revelations, had no formal journalism training. He had a more open and transparent way of reporting which gave weight to readers' comments and responses to his articles. It allowed him to garner the best and most insightful feedback, get new story ideas, make corrections that readers spotted, and add new information and sources as he went along. Greenwald became part of the process and he didn't presume to know everything. He's not "in" the news he writes, but he's part of it, and he grew a very commanding following with this newish brand of journalism.

The Correspondent, a membership-funded news website, is famously known for "unbreaking the news" because its approach is based around the idea that its journalists crowdsource ideas that merit further investigation from its members. Their daily dealings are open and transparent and members are invited to participate in the process.

The Internet has tinged the journalistic process, and the outcomes are direct and open communication. Being open and transparent leads to more trust among readers. More personal and authentic journalism is emerging in which journalists insert themselves and become part of the story.

A journalist can still be dispassionate in their piece while harnessing the tools at their disposal to garner feedback and sourcing the crowd to adjust, improve and enhance their work. The crowd sometimes has deeper insight into the subjects than the journalist, and acknowledging that is a source of journalistic strength.

Not all publications call for this sort of personable journalism and they may instead leave the first person perspective to the opinion columns. First person blurs the lines between mere "internet content" and a true scoop, the aim of which might be to unearth something novel and perspective-shifting that helps people make better decisions.

Journalists have to abide by the editorial policies of the publication they work at. For some editors, there is no place in a scoop with hard facts and information for the first person view. Editorial independence allows this restriction.

The worst offenders who tarnish journalism's reputation are liars such as the previously decorated German reporter Claas Relotius who wrote for *Der Spiegel* and *The New York Times* journalist Jayson Blair. Both were outed for fabricating stories and sources. These characters are far and few between but end up being sensational. No matter how good the checks and balances within a news organisation, fraud can slip through the cracks. Editors should consider that even star journalists are not above rigorous fact-checking and editing and never should be.

Fakery like that of Blair and Relotius makes editors nervous about personal stories, lest autobiography descend into fiction. But that doesn't have to be the outcome. In addition to the sort of personable work that Greenwald does, there's another more delicate instance when a journalist's own personal experience becomes the investigation. That's what de Vrieze and his wife faced as journalists following the birth of their stillborn child.

De Vrieze was looking for answers to why his child was stillborn. Doesn't the Netherlands have some of the most advanced prenatal care in the world? Why and how could this happen?

Getting their story published was difficult, precisely because they had a strong position, given their intimate involvement. Some editors shied away because it was hard for the couple to provide a balanced and nuanced view on the matter. They were forced to move to another newspaper midway through reporting. In fact, the story nearly didn't get published as a scoop but as an opinion piece, which is not what de Vrieze was looking for.

Being the main witness to the story forced de Vrieze to make sure all his facts were bulletproof. He found an editor who believed in them, worked tirelessly to even the tone and helped them to remain as dispassionate as possible about the story and where the reporting took them.

He said: "If you're very clear about your perspective and about your goals and open about your methods and about your sources and you are also talking to people that are not supporting that, and open to criticism from others, then it's okay. It's an illusion that you would otherwise be objective."

De Vrieze also pinpointed that an emerging strand of journalism favours transparency, which makes the journalist part of the process. In de Vrieze's case, the methods were more traditional but the perspective unique. A typical newspaper would have assigned a reporter to do the job for de Vrieze.

De Vrieze's case is extreme. Usually journalists put aside their perspective on the subject or only use it as a storytelling tool, if it helps characterize a person, insert a factoid or more generally add color to the story.

The conventional journalism that kept reporters out of the story is slowly eroding as the Internet calls for more transparency and readable content. Today, the journalist increasingly becomes part of the process, or even the heart of the story, while still being fact-based and balancing.

Having a first-person perspective in stories has always been part of the storytelling toolkit, but fact-based and hard-nosed news scoops call for it very rarely.

Just as journalists shouldn't become the story, they probably should not be chasing the latest, shiniest gadget. Yet the Internet has forced the return to a culture that journalism has already once fought to overcome. News on the Internet is the crowdsourced tabloid of its day.

Tabloids, so named because of the way their smaller paper size forced publishers to condense news, often favoured the salacious over the substantiated as low-cost printing brought news to the masses. Today, "tabloid" is synonymous with what became known in the US as "yellow press" in the early 20th century, which published and embellished stories to sell papers. You may have heard the expression "if it bleeds it reads," which is as much about what sold papers to make money as is it about sensationalism.

Don't get me wrong, I don't object to tabloids per se, as long as they follow some journalistic codes of conduct. Bates, whom I interviewed for this book, writes for the *Daily Mail*, a newspaper that quite easily fits the tabloid moniker. Tabloids regularly land scoops in a way that big, fancy and elitist broadsheets don't. Tabloids are mass products read by millions of people, and tabloid journalists have relationships with sources that the out-of-touch broadsheet can't always reach. They champion a different set of readers who have certain views and concerns, and there is value in that.

In fact, as the journalist Ron Rosenbaum notes in *The New New Journalism*, tabloid stories have "deeper dimensions, higher levels, passions—the same elements that inspire great art. After all isn't *Anna Karenina* on one level an adultery-suicide tabloid story?" (I love this description. Call me a *Kulturbanause* (philistine) if you like.)

The editors of the day were of the mind that nothing should stand in the way of a good story. Sometimes that meant stories needed to be made more exciting, so media producers would embellish small insignificant facts, like changing the hair color of the victim from a brunette to a redhead. They did worse, too, like invent scenes of war which were then sold as fact. With the power of the printing press in the hands of a few fierce competitors, outright fabrication and sensationalism trumped exactitudes.

Papers had a gatekeeper role and, given their ability and power to inform and educate the public, they began to take this role seriously. That role put editorial choices at the forefront of journalism with editors and journalists deciding what was newsworthy. This filter gave gatekeepers some power in deciding which version of the truth to present and a lens through which to see the world.

The golden age of that gatekeeper role has now been obliterated by the consolidation of publications under a few corporations and the appetite of those owners for political influence, and the web. What tabloids and the yellow press did in their heyday was clunky and slow. The fake news and clickbait we have today is fast and unstoppable. For someone who cares about the truth, the online spread of disinformation feels like an ocean oil spill with all its damaging, hard-to-clean-up and depressing effects.

Clickbait aims for virality; it's about reach and clicks on the web. Shocking celebrity tales, useless listicles, unsubstantiated conjecture and vacuous gossip are published to generate traffic. We love fun, lurid, scandalous, shocking and sometimes violent half-truths. That emotional propensity from the days of *Anna Karenina* and tabloid journalism hasn't changed.

We are drawn to shock and awe, as it feeds on primordial human desires and emotions. We fail to make a clear distinction that sensationalism— what we sometimes refer to as "the news"—isn't journalism.

Wijnberg hit the nail on the head when he said news is "sensational, exceptional, current events." Nothing more and nothing less. Some of these events become important to the historical record, but many serve no purpose other than being sensational, exceptional and current.

Think of every single Instagram post on your feed as fitting this precise description. On the web everything has become sensational, exceptional and current so that it's hard to tell what is real and what is folklore, satire or just plain fake.

The web ushered in a new culture of dealing with facts and fictions. This culture has further undermined journalism's credibility, as serious journalism competes with a flood of information posing as news.

ITERATE TO OBLITERATE

Iterative journalism is a form of discursive journalism that has developed on the web. Its discursive nature also means more intimacy with the reader, which is great, but its big downside is a lax approach to dealing with facts.

On the web, news updates can be pushed immediately, so a blogger or reporter is under pressure to get the story out, often before the facts can be properly scrutinized. *If it's wrong*, a blogger might tell themselves, *just run a correction or update, don't admit you got it wrong, gloss it over and move on. Nobody will notice or care, and if they do, they'll quickly forget.*

I wasn't aware of what it meant to issue a correction until working at a newswire. At most newswires this isn't taken lightly, and at *Bloomberg*, too, having to put CORRECTION in the headline is a blemish on your record as a reporter. If those blemishes add up, consider your job security under threat. Corrections need to be avoided at all costs.

If you do make a factual error, owning up to it is a matter of pride and integrity, for both you and your newspaper. You have to say: *Hey, we got it wrong.* You can't get away with just updating or fixing the story behind-the-scenes. Online, there is no corrections column like in the newspaper days, so the headline itself needs to show that the text below was altered. It's a serious matter.

I'm not talking about dotting an i or crossing a t. A correction is what might be termed a "material break": a factual error has occurred that requires the record to be put straight. This update offers a clarification or correction beneath the headline.

A lot of what is published on the web today doesn't hold itself accountable to those standards. Some publications might have editorial quality guidelines designed to prevent them from transmitting a hoax, fake news or plagiarized material—but, even so, once factual inconsistencies are out, it is often too late. What comes first often sticks, indefinitely.

THE UGLY STICKS

As Ryan Holiday writes in *Trust Me, I'm Lying: Confessions of a Media Manipulator,* citing a case in which a story was published without proper fact-checking, that first story takes on the mantle of truth even if denials and corrections follow. "They could never undo what they'd been accused of—no matter how spurious the accusation—they could only deny it. And denials don't mean anything online," he writes.

The original story in question gained a whopping 333,000 views, whereas a small 40-word correction of the original article was seen only 10,000 times, he points out. Beyond the factual error, the writer in question didn't follow a top-tier journalist's standards for fact-checking, give a chance for all parties to comment, nor take all necessary steps to ensure the story was accurate and ultimately true.

Lax editorial standards are the norm. Anyone can post anything; re-sharing falsehoods is easy if individuals don't scrutinize sources; and politicians and companies take control of the conversation themselves by pushing stories over social or high-traffic blogs, thereby co-opting the storyline to create new, alternative narratives.

Kellyanne Conway, an adviser to President Trump, famously coined the term "alternative facts" in an attempt to spin a television interview in favour of the US President. A photograph showed fewer people at

President Trump's inauguration than at former President Barack Obama's. In response the White House press secretary, Sean Spicer, gave a briefing claiming that Inauguration Day subway ridership in Washington, D.C. had been higher for President Trump than for President Obama. The picture alone, however, spoke volumes, and Conway's spin went beyond any real facts into the world of fiction, with Conway defending a falsehood.

"Alternative facts" are often the machinations of companies, marketeers and politicians—separately or collaboratively—with an agenda to coerce people into buying their products or voting for them. In this melange of megaphones, media organisations too are often seen as profit-machines, selling the sensational to make money.

Empowered by the web, they can broadcast their own messages instantly. And, without an incentive to fact-check themselves, they are faster than news organisations. Putting out false information may ultimately gain them more attention, because when journalists or other investigators try to show that the information is wrong, fake or one-sided, they unwittingly amplify the original message. Anything that is repeated tends to stick in the listener's imagination, even when it is repeated in the context of a fact-check.

By being first, individuals, companies and governments are taking control of the storyline and journalism is left to report it, often without the ability to control the outcome. A follow-up may provide context and clarification, but often what comes first sticks.

The problem is journalists are forced to report what politicians and companies are saying and to scrutinize that. In doing so, they become complicit in giving voice to the same people who are trying to control the story, even if that information is factually incorrect.

We are treading water in a sea of fake news, clickbait, half-truths and a me-first culture. The hallmarks of that culture feed certain pockets of a journalism culture that prides clicks over truth.

Iterative journalism, the more discursive online type that favors speed over accuracy, may be legitimate in some instances. Unfortunately, not everyone is trained in fact-finding or cares about journalistic code of conduct. Often the pressure to report forces the information to be published before a full fact-check can be run. It's a dangerous approach which leaves the door open to quick corrections and altered narratives that sow more confusion.

"It is as jumpy as reporters can get without outright making things up. Only the slightest twitch is needed for a journalist to get a story live," Holiday writes. "The pressure to 'get something up' is inherently at odds with the desire to 'get things right.'"

Even lofty editorial guidelines can't prevent individual journalists from making poor decisions. It doesn't matter how reputable the news organisation is: Blair and Relotius are a case in point and neither of these sordid tales are pretty. A handful of high-profile liars chose personal gain over the collective desire to maintain journalism's reputation; they corrupted and tarnished the profession's core. They stand out, rightfully so, because the majority of journalists do honest-to-god reporting. Most journalists fight the good fight.

Beyond the terrible transgressions of a few, journalists often stretch meanings or swallow a public relations (PR) line without running a proper check. Mostly it's just negligence, distraction, or rush, not ill intent, but it can cause serious damage. I too have unintentionally lost investors money with the click of a button and an honest mistake.

COMING CLEAN

As a *Bloomberg* reporter you are tasked with sending out headlines, which is a neat way to follow a press or conference call or public event. Imagine a series of bullet-points trickling down your screen. A headline is a smart abbreviation; it's like one point in a speech or a quote paraphrased in around 60 characters (you heard right, only 60, and this predates Twitter).

As reporters, we have a standard procedure to send out headlines during major events. The days are sometimes arranged around these events, with one ear in the presentation, and the other half of the brain trying to work out the right words to use in a headline.

Journalists regularly send out headlines *during* corporate conference calls with senior management of a variety of billion-dollar stock market listed companies. (We can always flesh out a full story later if what the CEO says is compelling enough.) In this way, newswire headlines beat Twitter at its own game before Twitter became a thing, I might add. From the organization's perspective, being "first" is the objective of writing these headlines.

Bloomberg headlines sometimes don't make sense to people who don't use the terminal. Even expert *Bloomberg* users are sometimes bewildered, as journalists don't always get it right. (Have a look at #strangebloombergheadlines on Twitter for a running collection of the bizarre). Beyond the occasional goof-ups, it's hair-raisingly tense if you're tasked with sending out these headlines, because people make or lose money based on what you write.

From the trader's perspective, they want to receive the information "first" so they can make the most profitable transactions. Traders' careers and fortunes are made on these short pieces of information. (They trade on the information contained in the headline because the headline is coded and certain codes signal potential trades, which in this day-and-age of automatic trading shouldn't surprise you.)

Headlines are a real-time affair so a reporter may shoot off several a minute—or none, if the speaker or event wasn't newsworthy. (What is newsworthy is at the discretion of the reporter, who should know what the heck is going on most of the time and what is potentially market-moving.)

On one particular day, I was one minute late to dial in to a company call and caught the tail end of a comment made by the chief financial officer. I sent out a headline, as what he said seemed significant, and the company's bond took a multimillion-dollar hit. Because I had missed the first minute, I misinterpreted the comment out of context—he had been speaking hypothetically! Published as fact, the statement did some serious damage. Luckily a shrewd trader messaged me to provide the accurate context and, going back over the transcripts, the newsroom issued a correction, but by that time, the damage had been done. The point is, in a world dominated by those who report first, the pressure to make sure the information gets out fast can lead to human error.

Unlike Relotius and Blair, I wasn't intentionally misleading anyone. I made a mistake, and I owned up to that mistake. I didn't hide but faced the consequences. The pressure of the job and feeling on top of things can spiral out of control. As a reporter, you know you should never send out a headline if you're unsure of its accuracy. When in doubt, leave it out and don't compromise accuracy for speed.

Even the best of us sometimes come to the job with a certain level of confidence and then just fire away, as I did. Was it my overconfidence, fear, or ignorance? I was late to the call and assumed I knew what was going on; that was my mistake.

Often these mistakes are not visible and go unnoticed, but first impressions tend to stick and are then hard to correct. That's why we have to prevent faulty information from making its way into the public domain in the first place. The ugly sticks, money is lost and journalistic records sullied.

SO MANY LIES

President Trump's rise to power had the pleasant side-effect of people flocking to *The New York Times* and other outlets because they yearned for context and understanding. The president himself is happy to make his own comments on Twitter, and, for the newspapers, it's easy to echo every Trump-tweet to generate traffic.

As a result, *The New York Times* has been more frequent in its mention of Trump compared to other Presidents at the height of their terms, as the *Columbia Journalism Review* reported. This is unfortunate because it draws attention to him; it's free publicity and amplifies the misinformation and falsehoods he propagates.

Reporters don't take our choice of words lightly, so, when a world leader disregards not only the truth but language itself, it sends most journalists into a tailspin.

Many journalists have fact-checked Trump's statements on the fly during or after the President's major speeches. Yet we don't really hear him being called an outright liar. Why is that? It's not only vexing but seriously annoying that reporters have to be cautious about calling him a liar, calling out specific falsehoods rather than using the big-L word.

A lot of what the President says may be factually incorrect but the bar is high for a lie: a false statement made intentionally. Does he intend to deceive, or is he just ignorant? Incidentally, behind the scenes we are more inclined to call him an idiot.

As Daniel Dale, the former Washington bureau chief of the *Toronto Star*, cleverly stated:

"In some cases, it's safe to say Trump is intentionally trying to deceive. In other cases, it's far less clear that he's being wrong intentionally— because, with Donald Trump, you regularly can't rule out the possibility that he is confused or ignorant.

If we journalists are going to present ourselves as arbiters of truth, we have to stick to what we know is true. And that means not calling something a lie when we don't have a reasonable certainty that Trump's intention is deception."

The issue of lying aside, Trump is polarizing. Left-leaning publications tend to fact-check him and are incentivized to do so to support their reader's views. On the flip side, right-leaning Trump-supporting publications have a propensity to ignore some falsehoods, focus on other facts and highlight what excites their readership.

Good journalism aims for getting the facts right and balancing the views of both parties on those facts with transparency. However, no publication wants to say that Trump could be right about *this* while being wrong about *that*, that he lied but he's still got a good point hidden in there somewhere. There is no excitement in a measured response like that and it's confusing!

But recognising the value of balance and transparency is key to understanding what you read as good journalism. Baseless and opinionated views won't be found in the scoop section of a publication.

Journalists are held to the highest standard and use of language. Even when it seems like a hindrance, it's the bedrock of reporting. Upholding that standard means we hold back (sometimes to a fault) on letting allegations fly freely. It doesn't mean we're trying to be objective to an impossible degree, like some would-be omnipotent know-it-all; this just means we speak with caution and accept our own subjectivity whilst striving for objectivity.

Codrea-Rado's story about the so-called "bunny hoarder" is a beautiful example of slashing the prevailing wisdom and putting more perspective on all the voices in a story. It's biased in the sense that it aims to cover the bunny keeper's perspective, something other news outlets were not doing. That also meant, while other outlets jumped to calling her a hoarder—which suggests a different bias!—Codrea-Rado had to tread more lightly.

"When it comes to kind of putting a label on someone, particularly when it's around a mental health issue, you have to be very clear in whether or not that person thinks that they have that particular illness or label or whatever it is you're trying to say of them," she said. "I asked her: does she think she's a hoarder? And she said, 'no.'"

Codrea-Rado forces a shift in perspective, inviting the reader to carefully consider the question of hoarding, which is a serious mental issue. She doesn't just treat the situation as a case of animal abuse, although some of the factual evidence supports that conclusion. Seen from the bunny keeper's perspective, she's giving these otherwise sentenced-to-death rabbits a life and home and doesn't see it as mistreatment at all.

Here's the more vexing thing about journalism which I didn't really understand before researching this book. You can still hunt for someone's personal truth and be both balanced and transparent. No journalist is ever totally objective and this is unavoidable. Codrea-Rado's story is clearly tipped in favor of one untold truth. That's part of what makes it so compelling and informative.

The way in which facts are presented will expose biases, and that's not a bad thing. In doing so, you are offering the best version of the truth you have managed to unearth. Nothing is ever complete but you'll try to achieve the closest thing to that. This is not journalism of fabrication (like tabloids of yesteryear), opinion or an experience-based approach (like personal essays). It's open, transparent and honest in its approach and delivery.

Singh's article on illegal mining started out with the perspective of the people most affected by the illegal activities. She's an environment reporter and social activist and doesn't hide the bias; she's open about it.

Wallace's story about racial bias in the small town of LaGrange cuts to the heart of activism on behalf of marginalised communities. Activism is part of why Wallace became a journalist to begin with.

"I would certainly say that I'm motivated by my own desire to make the world a better place and to amplify the voices of other people who are working to make the world a better place," Wallace told me.

Wallace dives deeper into the issue of objectivity in his book *The View from Somewhere*. Suffice to say, objectivity is impossible to obtain. We need to embrace and acknowledge our misgivings and our biases, be they liberal, Christian or otherwise.

This is at the heart of what motivates most journalists. If we see wrongdoing, corruption, marginalization of communities or the man-made destruction of our planet, for example, why wouldn't we work towards exposing injustices?

In the case of climate change, there is no denying the science any longer and *The Guardian* takes a clear stance. It's not "climate change," it's a "climate crisis," and the publication has amended its style guide to reflect that conviction. It's open about how and why it uses the words "climate crisis" and "climate denier."

"The OED (Oxford English Dictionary) defines a sceptic as 'a seeker of the truth; an inquirer who has not yet arrived at definite conclusions'. Most 'climate sceptics', in the face of overwhelming scientific evidence, deny climate change is happening, or is caused by human activity, so 'denier' is more accurate," *The Guardian* explained in removing the term "climate sceptics" from its reporting vocabulary.

When publications, just like *The Guardian*, decide to change the way journalists describe what we've known as "climate change" to the more pressing "climate crisis," "global heating" or "climate emergency," or when they ask to tell it like it is by talking about "climate sceptics" as "climate deniers," they are undeniably taking a stance for what they believe in.

To me, this means that journalists have social commitments. They seek to put an end to the world's wrongs. They may not directly advocate for solutions, but they follow threads, provide information, and identify scenarios for people to make a choice.

The same will go for conservative media in the US, who have a staunch belief in Christian orthodoxy and its morals and ethics. It is fine for "conservatives" to disagree with *The Guardian*'s choice to use the term "climate crisis" as long as conservative views are openly and transparently communicated and their validity contested. If a position is successfully contested, people should change their behavior and admit error: *Well, we got it wrong.*

"I think marginalized and oppressed people in particular have always been at the forefront of journalism that says 'this is how things could be' or as 'how things are that shouldn't be'," Wallace told me. "Status quo reporting normalized slavery when we had slavery."

This means that journalists themselves need to examine their own beliefs regularly to find out where they stand. For any scoop, it seems apparent that knowing your angle and bias are key to reporting that will attempt to balance out those inadequacies in the best way possible. Failing that, transparent reporting will shed light on the misgivings.

To end where we began, journalists themselves are sometimes the problem. As Janet Malcolm writes in *The Journalist and the Murderer*: "any journalist who's not too stupid and not full of himself will know that what he does is morally indefensible."

It's a harsh criticism but one that journalists need to be aware of in our own conscience. What is the driving motivation behind the work? If we are operating for personal financial gain, maybe our own motivations are tarnished in a way that compromises how we choose to report the issue?

It's hard not to feel like a confidence trickster at times. The only way to overcome that is to cultivate self-awareness, even if it's uncomfortable. *Why am I trying to get this person or source to open up, why do I want them to speak? What is my gain?*

Self-awareness and the blind pursuit of the story will intersect in an unpleasant way at some point and it is in those moments that brutal—in fact, radical—honesty is needed. By saying *I'm unsure, I don't know, I'm conflicted,* we can maintain both our integrity and sense of purpose.

This might also be the greatest limit of journalism, as it can't truly get to the bottom of that which requires personal reflection and awareness. Dobelli, in his essay "Avoid News," is more scathing in his attack of some journalists' ignorance, but separates the wheat from the chaff by acknowledging that good journalists "take time" with their stories, check their facts and think things through.

"But like any profession, journalism has some incompetent, unfair practitioners who don't have the time—or the capacity—for deep analysis," he writes. "Some reporters copy from each other or refer to old pieces, without necessarily catching up with any interim corrections. The copying and the copying of the copies multiply the flaws in the stories and their irrelevance."

(Many professions are plagued by charlatans but also have conscientious practitioners. This isn't a novel concept or idea, yet I, too, am "copying," leaning on Dobelli to support the truth of this statement.)

Often journalists are drawn to writing about an event that is timely because the "current event" offers a peg, something to pin it on. Timeliness manufactures a kind of temporary relevance. Readers may feel they've learned something valuable. The story flows from this "current event" peg, rather than from broad, deep relevance to anything permanent, just because the topic is hot.

Journalism will try to obtain facts, explain the news, provide context and shed light. It will scrutinize the facts and put them to the test, examine the source and be as transparent as possible. Ignoring the facts is a recipe for disaster. Attention to the facts should be the most important consideration.

As Alan Rusbridger, the former editor-in-chief of *The Guardian*, notes so succinctly in *Breaking News: The Remaking of Journalism and Why it Matters Now:* "The truth can only follow on from agreed facts. Facts can only be agreed if they can be openly articulated, tested … and contested. That process of statement and challenge helps something like the truth to emerge. From truth comes progress. In the absence of this daylight, bad things will almost certainly happen."

Good journalists are able to let go of the dream of being first and will take the extra time to get it right. To overcome the constraints of being first, journalism needs to be investigative in nature but it will also inform how the journalist acts. Intentions matter. Journalistic rigour matters. Morally defensible actions to get at the truth—in both personal affairs and in the name of a story—matter.

To get at the scoop, you must first conduct a search and that search matters.

Trust, Idiots and Stones

Following your curiosity is a great beginning, and a relentless pursuit of unanswered questions will take you through to a scoop's conclusion. To get to those answers you need people and not the Internet.

Sure, the Web is a good starting place, but there is more useless than useful information out there. The volumes of quick-fix stories, marketing chatter, miscellaneous "content," and noise make it difficult to get to the heart of a matter. It's a great resource, but a real scoop will eventually require some leg-work.

"When I'm coming up with ideas, I need to talk to the top experts in a field, people who are deeply immersed in an area. I zero in on that person because he or she can tell me, in a nutshell, what is really new and exciting in the field," as Richard Preston says in *The New New Journalism*.

Even data-journalists, whom you might assume are desk-bound, have to make phone calls, meet and talk to people about the data they are accessing and verify that what they have found out is accurate in the real world.

Buzzfeed's *Hidden Spy Planes* data journalism project, which used machine learning to uncover which planes were surveillance or spy planes, wasn't without fault. It incorrectly identified skydiving planes as spy planes—an error that came to light once realities were checked on the ground.

In fact, it's the facts.

A drive to represent marginalized communities, show the effects of climate change on peoples, or fact-check a company's business practices will earn you a scoop. The type of story you are looking for will determine the type of source network you're going after and how you'll approach these sources.

For a mergers and acquisitions reporter, the rules of engagement are high-octane. There is a set of unspoken rules that you learn as time goes by. A lot of the reporting involves people with whom you have to build relationships and earn trust by sweet-talking or giving information you know they value. The flow of information is important and you play a part in keeping it flowing for them.

Reporting is something you learn by doing. Necessity will teach you how to talk to a source who has signed a non-disclosure agreement. You must become a fish in the water, swimming with the school of people you are hoping to understand and write about.

A company source told me that some of the biggest, fanciest labs in the world still used pencils and paper to collect data. Really, I thought? When I imagined scientists, I imagined novelty and science fiction. I didn't believe that scientists still used pencils, so I pulled in a colleague to investigate the ways in which scientists behaved "backwardly."

The "mechanism" for getting to your source will be different, as Leon Dash, the Pulitzer Prize-winning journalist, notes in *The New New Journalism*. For his eight-part series "Rosa Lee: A Mother and Her Family in Urban America," his introduction to adolescent pregnant girls couldn't come from the head of the church's youth council. Instead, it had to come from another sixteen-year-old girl, he noted.

Building trust starts with getting the right introduction.

TRUST IS EARNED

As the saying goes, it's not what you know but who you know. When covering communities and people you know nothing about, or very little about, you'll need the right introductions to get as close as possible to the subject.

Reporting momentum builds with the trust you earn from the first one or two people in the community. Word goes around that you mean no harm and that you belong. Sometimes, as was the case in Ross's coverage of the Christian communities he reports on, a source keeps returning to you with more ideas and fodder for scoops.

There is an invisible line you cross at which point how you behave becomes equally as important as who you know. Like a method actor, you begin walking and talking like those you cover. At some point your knowledge may pass that of an expert, not in depth, but in breadth. By riding the coattails of curiosity, facts, knowledge and cultural understanding, your knowledge of the community or group of people you are covering will emerge organically and you gain a more holistic view.

In business journalism, reporters make acquaintances fast. Gaining trust is easier because it's the name of the game. Business is built on trust; money is a piece of paper built on trust. Not all communities are as easy to cover. Some journalists must go undercover.

Alikaj risked life and limb to go undercover into an area of Albania ravaged by illegal logging. He needed proof on the ground, which he found by chaperoning locals, but he wouldn't have gotten access without the connection provided to him.

In a longer-term investigation, Ted Conover went to the heart of Sing Sing, New York's maximum-security facility, as a guard. He spent a number of years living and working there to provide an elaborate inside look into the US prison system from a unique and untold perspective of these prison guards.

IGNORANCE IS BLISS

Beyond the importance of blending in, the hidden secret to a journalist's success is their total and complete openness, and in some instances—at least initially—their ignorance about the people and communities they cover.

Ignorance about the subject gives them space for curiosity, creativity, and learning. And, especially when they admit their ignorance to themselves, they will tend to maintain certain kinds of neutrality and reserve judgement for later.

Journalists tend to remain free of judgement during the reporting phase. I'm skeptical of anyone who knows the outcome of the story they set out to write. Doesn't a preconceived conclusion seem at odds with the idea of "reporting it out"?

Only once sufficient information has been collected can a journalist begin to make decisions about how the information is organized and presented. It is at this stage that biases, preferences and storytelling warp the material into a complete and understandable universe for the reader.

From the community-based journalist, to the slow passive observer who spends days with their subject, to the fast and furious financial reporter under deadline and all shades in-between, each journalist has their own tactics to get people to open up. How fast people open up will depend on the story and subject they are covering. How well you understand the people in these communities—whether it's black urban mothers or bankers in London's Mayfair—you'll need to learn their language.

Is this part acting? I've certainly felt like an actor at times, but always in a truthful manner, in much the way that we "put on an act" or simply feel self-conscious when making a new acquaintance. Making polite, goal-directed conversation is different from lying. I'm not going to pretend to have a Maserati in my garage (because I don't) just to impress a banker. Instead, I focus on relatable, universal experiences, like family, sports and entertainment, that offer plenty of templates to connect with.

This is generally the greatest problem most of us have in getting anything done as journalists. People don't know who we are and don't feel they can trust us. Many people have never had to work with a journalist before or been confronted by them if they are not in positions of power.

Oftentimes journalists start out small, at publications with little name-recognition, churning out reams of copy on tight deadlines. Not always the best for deep reporting, but good for developing skill and a reputation. Eventually, if you're working for an outlet like *Bloomberg*, your access to high-level executives and other sources is easier because, as a media organization, its serious reporting credentials have proven that they value speed, accuracy and fact-based reporting.

The community about which you write needs to understand the reach and power of the media organization you work for. You hitch a ride on that reputation which is easier to maintain than build yourself.

Wallace's knock-out story on unpaid fines being pushed through utility bills was not only bad for residents generally, it reeked of racial discrimination. The local politician didn't take a stand or make a statement. Instead the city's lawyer sent a canned statement by email which was a frustrating let-down.

To reprint the response was Wallace's duty but he was not native to that town. Given more time—and especially money, presumably—he could have revealed even more of the deep fabric of socio-economic discrimination in LaGrange. He didn't have the full weight of a well-funded newsroom behind him at the time, but that didn't discourage him, either.

Don't let the size of your publication deter you from an investigation that you find worthy of your time. In the absence of transparency and balance—where a key player doesn't want to speak—whatever statement you are able to get from other parties will have to suffice. The onus is on them, as long as you have done everything in your power to include their views.

When you write that a key player refused to comment for your story, the reader can see their noncompliance, and they will judge that behavior on its own merits. The most you can do is make every effort to be transparent about what you are writing and reporting on.

On the flip side, a local publication with name recognition might get you a local scoop nobody else is chasing or cares about. As with Alikaj, whose fluency in Albanian helped him get access, being "a local" will inevitably take you closer to the action. Think about what knowledge or skill you have that makes you an insider where you already are.

So before you despair about not having access to the biggest names, look closer to home, and find people locally to help you build credibility. As de Vrieze experienced, sometimes the story is at your doorstep, and covering your own community doesn't require access to politicians, celebrities or YouTubers with glitzy PRs and gatekeepers.

KEEP IT SIMPLE

To get what you want you'll go as far down the rabbit hole as you have to. For some of the greatest projects that means years; for others, that means just enough to meet the story deadline. The point is, in a lot of the cases above, you'll just need to understand how basic things function and to get your facts straight.

A lot of what journalists do is just understand, interpret, and express things in a way that makes them relatable to a wider audience. I ask myself whether my Mom would understand what I have written. If she can understand my ramblings, I'm on a good path to clarity and making myself understood.

For de Vrieze's story, that meant putting a host of complicated jargon into the right format for the broader newspaper audience he was addressing. His background in biomedical sciences helps him communicate the science to his readers. It's easier for the average reader to get lost, which is why oftentimes scientists make poor communicators as they are too wrapped up in their work and the details, unlike de Vrieze who understands both the science and how to communicate it.

You usually don't need a degree to report within a subject area, but this sort of specialization can help. Alikaj has an advanced degree in geoinformatic engineering which may help him understand the logging industry a bit better. A journalist should go as far as is needed for their own understanding to communicate the issue clearly. I knew nothing about mergers and acquisitions or the pharmaceutical industry and ended up covering both. It just means you're going to learn those beats and industries fast, and sometimes immersion is the best teacher.

If you don't understand something, make every effort to find out more. Peel back more layers. If you lose interest, maybe you weren't that curious to begin with or you've satisfied your thirst for understanding? It happens.

I feel that way about drug development, something I too covered as a reporter. We used to agonize over which word to choose to describe this or that "mechanism of action," a fancy term for how-the-drug-works-in-the-body. Once I'd grasped a basic working understanding of these processes, I wasn't willing, curious, nor did I have enough time to dig deeper into the science, even though I knew just enough to get the science across. I didn't have the time or scope to dig deeper without actually studying the science, and I had reached my limits. De Vrieze's reporting was exceptional not only because you can see that he has a deep understanding of the science but he also gives the reader enough of an understanding to make sense of the issue at-large.

A great example of getting to the bottom of something which ultimately unlocks your understanding of a particular phenomenon is something Malcolm Gladwell also beautifully illuminates in his story "The Treatment." The story talks about the importance of the Kaplan-Maier curve in cancer research.

You don't need to be a cancer researcher to understand the Kaplan-Maier curve. This simple chart, Gladwell explains, is what will essentially make or break whether a cancer drug will ever make it to market. That's it. Having identified its importance, Gladwell has given the reader enough background to guess whether a cancer drug might work and therefore to be enthralled by its promise.

You don't need to understand the mechanics of how to gather, render and produce the Kaplan-Maier statistics. You only need to understand its function and use, and that's a shortcut (before going out and getting a degree in medicine!) to understanding what's at stake.

LEAVE NO STONE UNTURNED

Your job is to find out everything there is to know about the situation you are investigating.

As Lise Olsen, an investigative reporter at *The Texas Observer* said in a recent online course on investigative journalism: "Look for big fat liars." It's not just people's statements you should be trying to check, it's the people themselves and all the information in the story. "And that's part of what our mission is, an investigative reporter is trying to figure out what is being hidden and why it is being hidden."

Bates's investigation into the Jeffrey Epstein case threw up a host of unresolved questions that were being ignored by the courts. He took it upon himself to look very deeply into the case and connect the dots where the courts didn't want to, or couldn't.

The sheer volume of facts involved in a story like this means there will be volumes of smaller investigations you will need to do to corroborate and substantiate those facts.

In the story I did for *Businessweek* on digital labs, I spoke to a scientist and a lab technician who described in detail how they conducted their work. This conversation was only to substantiate claims that technicians at best used manual spreadsheet tools to gather and collect data and at worst were still recording processes manually with a pencil and paper. The truth was more nuanced; as it turned out, some of the equipment was spitting out spreadsheets but lab technicians collected and collated data from these spreadsheets manually.

Our editor asked very specific questions about how a lab technician collected the data, asking whether she had to put the data on USB jump-drives or whether she could digitally send them from the lab into a central location and then work on presenting the findings. We had to investigate every detail. How much time did it take? Was this a problem? How did it actually all take place? All these questions needed to be answered so that we could have an accurate and clear picture.

Every number we used in the piece needed to be located and checked off in the final draft. Each name needed to be checked and double-checked with no room for factual inconsistency. These processes can take time, which delays publication.

This also means that you'll need to know more than your editor and be in a position to answer every question about the subject in a way that satisfies a graduate examination board. The more you know, and the faster you can access your sources, the quicker it will get done. During the process of your talks and research, you may acquire as much working knowledge as that of a graduate in a similar field, if your investigation is long and deep enough. If you've established a good relationship with the sources and can maintain it, expect to go back to them, time and time again, as new questions crop up.

Though trivial to the uninitiated, there are aspects of the final product of reporting that can't always be identified by the naked eye. These indicators distinguish a scoop from less rigorous and reliable stories and that's what I'll talk about in the next part of the book.

PART II

What makes a scoop
(and how to write one)

Do I have a scoop?

"Some brilliant reporters can't write. Some brilliant writers can't report. Some very able reporters report, but don't break news. Some news-breaking reporters can't see the bigger picture. Many thinking journalists aren't interested in reporting." —Alan Rusbridger, *Breaking News*

Many journalists on the job never write a single scoop. A journalist has a "scoop" when they are the first to report and exclusively cover a new revelation. This may bring prestige to the news outlet or, at the very least, sell a few more newspapers or get more page views. Sadly, most journalists don't get "the big one," but they may have something smaller that is nonetheless meaningful, and that's why new definitions are needed.

QUANTIFIABLE SCOOPS

When I get a scoop, I'm thrilled because its impact is undeniable.

A while back I got a tip-off that a public company was planning to sell off a major part of its business in an effort to unlock cash. I didn't recognize the company's name, so I looked up its stock market ticker and learned that it had a market capitalization of over $2 billion.

Usually, I have no idea why people in the know (aka "sources") share sensitive information with me. I have to be extremely careful, even if I've known the source for years. The information may not be true, and I have to find a way to independently verify it. I can't ask others directly, because sharing the information with the wrong person might implicate me in a crime or conspiracy (insider trading, for example, is illegal where I live).

In this case, I wasn't able to actively share the information but had to find other company insiders who could offer up the same information with enough prompts. If multiple people volunteered the same information, I could feel more confident that it was legit. This is tricky, really tricky. It sometimes feels like fencing with javelins, or jousting with words using unwieldy conversation techniques.

The company in question was about to sell a major division, one worth several million Euros. This type of event—just like production site closures, job cuts or the departure of senior management—can move a company's share price. Or it might not. What investors are willing to pay for the company stock depends on their expectations.

I did some basic research by pulling up the company's latest reports and presentations to see how much the business generated and to get a steer on its strategy. The potential sale wasn't reported yet. *I've got a scoop,* I thought. *I have information that no other outlet has and I'll be the first to report it.* I had the textbook definition of a scoop. I thought I had something more, too: My story would make a measurable impact on the world. The really tasty reward would be seeing the company's share price move after the story's publication. Then I'd know I had a scoop that mattered.

In reality, I may have had something smaller: What you might describe as a "scooplet." I may have been advancing a story, as Syed did in her story about Nestlé's skincare business, using a new shred of information that expanded on an already developing situation. Stories like Syed's are typical in financial journalism, which often means unearthing a new piece of information that in itself won't move the share price but has a subtle impact because investors are closely tracking each and every move a company might make. In Syed's case, the big scoop would have been to first report the sale of Nestlé's skincare business, not the follow up on who's bidding.

When the stock moves, it's measurable. Neat. Clean. A journalist can take it to their editors and show them and say, "Look what I did!"

NON-QUANTIFIABLE SCOOPS

Most scoops, though exclusive, aren't measurable. Are these lesser scoops?

- Getting the CEO on the line for an "exclusive"?
- Reflecting someone's perspective on a particular conflict?
- Scoring a shot or angle on a photograph which nobody else has?
- Unmasking a twisted healthcare system?
- Holding an industry or a government to account?

When I was covering the pharmaceutical company Roche, the company's CEO once used the word "stupid" to describe how cancer drugs were priced. Ironic, because Roche is party to the system that prices these drugs. The story didn't move Roche's share price, but it was a scoop nonetheless as it showed that this mild-mannered Swiss executive could lash out. In the insular world of drug development and investing, this mattered. We had it first and it was exclusive, so it was a scoop.

To be the first is extremely difficult in today's social media-driven age. Companies and individuals have the ability to communicate directly with the world via Twitter, Instagram and Facebook, preempting journalists with the click of a button. Think of President Trump's tweets about Lockheed Martin which wiped $4 billion off the aerospace company's share price. I never thought journalists would be writing stories about a President's tweet explaining how the two events—a tweet and a price change—correlated.

In the old days, before a US President initiated tweetstorms, a journalist may have been sitting in a briefing room, caught the president making the comment and then pushed it out as news to the public. The journalist's decision may have moved the needle. That power is gone, mostly. Companies and individuals regularly out-scoop journalists on being first, leaving them being beaten at their own game, instead aggregating official statements.

There have however been cross-border investigations led by multiple investigative teams across Europe who have had successes since the old days. The CumEx-Files unveiled how individuals and corporations were swindling European's taxpayers out of billions of Euros. The Panama Papers exposed offshore financial dealings that cost governments around the world billions of dollars. We never would have found out about the Facebook-Cambridge Analytica scandal which tarnished Facebook, and shed light on the issue of data privacy, without the work of journalists. Carole Jane Cadwalladr and *The Guardian*, among others, helped expose and make sense of how data was illegally harvested and used to try and swing a major US election. Then again, Julian Assange's WikiLeaks cut out the media middle-man but was a regular source of scoops for journalists who took time to sift through and make sense of all its revelations.

Big game reporting isn't over but it's tough and it's rare. Most people have heard of how Bob Woodward and Carl Bernstein's Watergate investigations played a crucial role in the resignation of then-US president Nixon. It was the golden age of journalism where print media had a monopoly on the scoop.

These big scoops shifted the public's attention, informed policy changes, forced politicians to step down, and exposed injustices in the world. Mostly in immeasurable ways that were hard to quantify, but their impact on public opinion is undeniable. So, if you, as a journalist, ever get the chance to work on something of this magnitude, consider yourself lucky, and get ready for the long haul.

Some journalists work on stories that affect communities on a smaller stage with a different power. Just like the Roche CEO's quip about the process for pricing drugs, a local issue may only matter to you if you're in that information habitat, the epicentre of a specific group of people's awareness.

Journalism impacts individuals and communities first.

If you think about Watergate, it's actually a local story with national significance. Many stories are like that. They require passionate journalists looking into all sorts of issues on their doorsteps.

Alikaj's story is a stand out example. Without his passion and connections, such local investigations into illegal logging in the beautiful forests of Albania may not have happened. His story had implications for Albania's bid to join the European Union.

That influence is tough to measure. Who read Alikaj's story? Who was outraged about the illegal activity and corruption? We can't measure the indirect influence of these stories.

Scoops are local and community-driven.

Scoops are exclusively reported and (oftentimes) consist of new pieces of information relating to a person, place or event previously unknown to a wider public. In reality a scoop also depends on the publication through which you view it.

As Staley suggests, news doesn't need to move markets and, in fact, *Quartz* assumes people get their breaking news elsewhere. In this environment, it's a scoop of conception or a scoop of ideas, unearthing something bubbling below the surface, that can shine through.

Staley thrust a long-standing failure of the pharmaceutical industry into the limelight by telling the story through the eyes of one biotech executive. He explained that the industry had made little progress on developing treatments for people who suffer strokes in part because the industry was not incentivized to do so. No other reporter or news publisher presented it to the world the way he did and that in itself was a scoop.

"I pieced together multiple strands of reporting from multiple places and braided them together into a narrative format that no one else had done before. The total is worth a lot more than the sum of the parts and that has value and we could think of that as a scoop," he said.

With this definition of a scoop, people get a deeper and richer understanding of the world around them. Staley's *Quartz* story is also unusually long at nearly 7,000 words and you come away learning a lot from reading it. Breaking news that squeezes information into less than one page can't always do that.

Scoops are rich, deep and thorough.

A scoop is simply getting the information to the people that need it to make decisions. This is what newspapers used to do, and what the 7 o'clock news delivered, in the most traditional sense. Journalists didn't always consider their "breaking news" to be "a scoop"; it was just the daily round up of what happened.

Now consider a scoop in an information-scarce environment. In Cameroon, for example, although the country is considered a democracy, most people don't even know when the next election might be held, so any information related to the basic functioning of its democracy is a scoop. As Atabong pointed out:

"The system is so bad that nobody knows what's going to happen next time, so when the journalist is privy to such information it's considered at the local level, like a scoop."

Scoops in information-poor environments tend to elevate journalism's purpose as it is needed for democracy. This results in positive views towards journalists. In information-rich democracies, people already have the basic information they need, so journalists tend to seek influence through damaging individuals and companies and end up being viewed more negatively. Reporting to cause harm doesn't always make a journalist look good but there are other types of scoops, such as those that offer a fresh perspective, that can balance the scales of what is often regarded as lopsided, negative reporting.

So what about breaking news in an information-rich environment such as New York?

Codrea-Rado's story on a bunny hoarder in New York would not, according to the above standards, be a scoop. It doesn't help anyone make more informed decisions, nor is the bunny hoarder's existence new information, as the general situation was already known before she wrote her story.

Codrea-Rado interviewed the bunny hoarder in question, and the result was a story about culture and society, not breaking news to turn the tide in an election or move a share price. Can this still be a scoop?

It can.

In Codrea-Rado's case, two things play in favour of it being a scoop. First, although the story was known, she took it international by having it re-told in *The Guardian*, a greater audience than the local New York City blogs where it originated. Secondly, she spoke to the one person nobody had managed to get on the line: the protagonist. It was exclusive. She went where others hadn't.

There are scoops that are small stories taken to a bigger platform by a journalist who's found local news of significance and takes it national. There are scoops of conception and perspective which are just as important as they shed light on a large issue, such as mental health and hoarding as a serious condition. Codrea-Rado produced coverage that ultimately yielded more transparency and balance.

Local stories called the woman a "hoarder," which is a serious mental condition, but they failed to ask her about how she sees things. The woman was saving bunnies from slaughter and did her best to give them a home according to the standards she considered just (although she lacked knowledge of the proper oversight and legal context as set by local standards). Arguably, the woman should have known better. Nonetheless, Codrea-Rado humanized her, gave her space to breathe, and let readers see her perspective.

Scoops provide new and untold perspectives.

If you haven't written any scoops yet, don't despair, as someone as seasoned and thorough as Codrea-Rado perceives herself as not having written any, either.

She told me: "In reality, unless you're a news reporter, you probably won't get a scoop. I don't think I've ever actually gotten a full proper scoop before in the sense that no one has ever written about it before."

In my interpretation, Codrea-Rado has indeed written a scoop, just not in a Watergate-way. It's a quieter, subtler form of scoop on a beat that requires just as much finesse as hard-hitting business and political news with fresh information.

It's not a scoop if at least some information worked up by a journalist isn't fresh. Old information can be retrieved through desk research. Fresh reporting requires that the journalist get out of their seat and talk to the people, scrutinize the documents, study the statements, corner the key witness and seek out the statistics to provide context and perspective. The story can then be presented either as "breaking news" or as a "follow-up investigation."

Scoops don't pretend to be anything other than investigations that, in some shape or form, get to the bottom of an issue deeply felt by the journalist who's investigating them.

How to get a scoop

"'Stumble' is the key word. So much of it is luck, not dumb luck, but a kind of informed good fortune. It's like panning for gold, you know what you're looking for, and you have a notion where to look and how to look for it, but whether you find it or not has everything in the end to do with chance." —Alex Kotlowitz, *The New New Journalism*

General ideas for your next story may come from an archive, a book or somewhere else, but the heart of the story—the real scoop—is more likely to come from your fellow human, so it's best to learn how to stumble into them.

The start of a good story and a scoop are the people you meet and interact with. These are either long-standing sources that you have built over time or through serendipity, bumping into the right person at the right time. There are ways and means to sniff out a good story if you're willing to follow your intuition.

Being a journalist is all about maximizing "soft skills," although I hate that word because it somehow implies they are weaker or lesser skills. Not at all! Communication, above all, is the cornerstone of anyone's work. You can't get a job if you don't have so-called soft skills. Let's face it, some people ride a wave to the top of the corporate hierarchy because they have soft skills. How you act on the job as a journalist is the cornerstone of generating scoops.

THE ROSS WAY

Ross has spent years in the Christian communities he covers. He has developed an intimate understanding of the people, is a faith-based person himself, and is deeply embedded in the communities of the Churches of Christ. His work is an outgrowth of his beliefs and he can get in close to the groups he serves with his work and investigations.

It should come as no surprise, then, that the source for "A Perpetrator in the Pews" was someone in the community, someone he had previously written a story on. Years back he had interviewed minister Jimmy Hinton whose own father was a minister and pedophile preacher. Ross had told Hinton's story, a twisted tale of a man who reported his own father to the police, sparking an investigation which eventually led to his father's sentencing. That coverage, and Ross's relationship with his source, were the foundation for "A Perpetrator in the Pews" which exposed a new scandal.

"For me that's always been a helpful way of getting stories... is to do one story. Jimmy's story was really close to him and it was really hard for him. But I spent time with him and got to know him and I think he appreciated the way I told his story," Ross said.

Hinton became a strong advocate for the victims of sexual abuse in the church, so he was tapped into what this group of people were talking about. Without Ross's relationship to Hinton, he may never have found out that church leaders were doing more than just turning a blind eye to a potential sexual predator in their midst, and were in fact enabling his presence in their church: the core idea in "A Perpetrator in the Pews."

Ross followed his instincts because he understood the grievances his sources expressed. He wouldn't have been tipped off without the long-standing relationship built around his work as an unfamiliar reporter on Hinton's case. The relationship developed naturally from there with Ross returning to Hinton regularly to check in. Above all, he did a thorough job on that first story and earned the minister's respect and trust.

Ross's approach shows how important it is to maintain a good relationship to people you interview for stories. It doesn't matter what beat you are on. Your objective should always be the same: keep a positive and professional relationship to people you speak with, even if you may never speak to them again. You never know where or what they may end up doing. If they like you, and know they can trust you, they might offer up scoops weeks, months or years later.

Ross's network delivers regular tip-offs but he can't chase them all. Years of coverage have led to his understanding of what is a standout and shocking revelation that might merit deeper investigation.

When you are starting out as a journalist, your networks are not in place and often you don't have time to wait for them to develop. With a bit of patience and care, though, you'll get closer to the people and become a valued and trusted member of the community.

Ross's sourcing is organic and community-based and above all he's been at it for years. We're not all that fortunate, but it's not the only way into a scoop. Sometimes you just walk right into them.

THE CURIOSITY SHOW

If you don't already have strong ties to a relevant community, get close to the people right in the middle of the action. That's the most direct approach.

Wallace and Singh had similar experiences. They both were on another assignment and ended up with an unexpected story with curiosity acting as their guide.

Wallace was traveling to Indiana to do a story about electronic ankle monitors on people being released from immigration detention. He planned to investigate how much money the ankle monitor companies were taking from the government. That in itself may have been a scoop right there, but he also learned something different during the investigation.

He was set to meet a local undocumented immigrant who had been made to wear one of these monitors in LaGrange, a small county in the midwestern state. The person who arranged this meeting told Wallace about a policy that lumped people's unpaid municipal fines (for minor misdemeanours) in with the municipal water bills. If fines weren't paid, utilities got shut off.

"My first reaction," he told me, "is one that a lot of people had to this story and was like, 'Are you serious?' It was like nothing I'd ever quite heard of. And then it turned out to be just, you know, verifiably true."

Make note of claims that get a double-take. If it seems odd, maybe it is nonsense—or maybe it's true? That's your cue to find out. When editors tell journalists to keep an ear to the ground, this is exactly what they mean. Wallace made a mental note of this odd policy.

It can take a bit of practice to recognize something's weird or off. Part of that skill is identifying the best sources, gaining their trust, and listening to them. Wallace talked to communities that already felt sidelined or marginalized. They were the ones experiencing the pain, and he listened closely and asked questions. He still had to check things out—you can't rely on the word of one person—and that quest could have led nowhere. In this case, though, he had success.

It's the moments in-between investigations that sometimes lead to the next scoop.

Singh was in Goa, India for an environment fellowship. She'd just finished up the work for that and had some time to spare when she walked into a protest against mining taking place in Goa's capital, Panjim.

"I was just simply curious to see why those protests were taking place. So literally it was going in, talking to the people who were staging the protest and one thing led to another."

Just let your own curiosity surprise and then guide you. Singh wasn't shy about her own ignorance on the matter, in fact, she tackled it by talking to people and figuring it out as she went along.

Sometimes you don't walk into the scoop all at once. Sometimes you have to pick up the phone multiple times.

DESKBOUND

Syed's scoop is sourced very differently from Wallace's or Singh's. She confesses that a lot of the reporting done for her Nestlé/Colgate story was done via the phone. Why do her sources pick up those calls in the heat of the moment, when a comment is needed in the span of a few minutes? Because she has previously been out wining and dining them, getting in "face-time" and making herself known to anyone and everyone involved in dealmaking.

She had already done all the hard work by developing those sources so they picked up immediately when she called about Nestlé/Colgate. She had earned their trust, a bit like Ross did with the communities he served. In the world of financial journalism, this trust can be earned faster as many of these actors understand how communication works in public markets.

CEOs, analysts, bankers and traders are trained by public relations professionals on what they can and cannot say. They are coached on how to take questions and on how to deflect and divert probes on information that might be considered secret. They are highly literate, particularly in ways that are relevant to their professions and areas of expertise. Some but not all of these characters (most notably CEOs, company reps and analysts, in this case), are encouraged to develop positive relationships with journalists to earn their respect and leverage a journalist's reach in times of need.

Small, local nonprofits may have a lot of specific knowledge but they may not understand "the media," which is more of an amorphous collection of hard-to-define-organizations with unclear agendas. There is a greater need for education upfront about what journalists do and why you should talk to one.

Syed, meanwhile, has spent time figuring out when her sources are on their lunch hours, when they are on the road in a taxi or on their way to work, or when they are leaving the office. As a result, she knows when to make that decisive call to catch them. She's agonized over people's mobile numbers, shooting them text messages to find out when it would be best to call.

Not only will your scoop live and die by the sources you can procure, it will live and die by the other journalists you can get to help you. No work is done in isolation. The best scoops require multiple journalists, with multiple sources working as a team to fill in the blanks.

"These kinds of potentially market-moving scoops require a huge amount of resources and teams to pull off because they are very secretive processes," Syed said.

Syed's access to a wide array of sources who are privy to inside information on a deal also requires the support of the newsroom journalism network. As the byline on her story goes to show, she relied on other bureaus to piece together the scoop she helped source.

In another example, Bates, based out of New York, tapped the *Daily Mail*'s picture research team in London for his story on Prince Andrew's connection to the Jeffrey Epstein case.

Bates spent time talking to paparazzi who used to work the French Riviera or at London's nightclubs. They gave him pictures that were then examined by the picture researchers at *The Daily Mail,* placing Prince Andrew with certain people central to the Epstein investigation.

Bates used court-related document access to consider relationships and events beyond those mentioned at trial. After identifying people who could potentially serve as key witnesses, he put public pressure on them to come forward in the investigation.

LUCK & GUTS

Oftentimes it is sheer luck and persistence that land you a scoop. There is really no recipe for that. Sometimes a whistleblower comes forward like Christopher Wylie in the Facebook-Cambridge Analytica scandal. All you can hope for is that you are at the right place at the right time: on-site, already knowing who's who, and able to pinpoint the offbeat comment or grab that person.

In Codrea-Rado's case, the story would have failed without comment from the protagonist. She spent time hanging around the woman's home, in the cold, ringing doorbells. Nobody answered, so she slipped her name and her number under the door. Lucky but also earned: she did what was in her power.

"I honestly thought, you know, she is not going to call me," she recalled. "And I kind of go, okay, the story is dead in the water. But I got home that evening and she texted me and agreed to talk."

In Wallace's case, he knew he had a story with the court fines and water bills. He just needed to find a citizen willing to talk about the issue and provide him with further evidence. So he went back out to LaGrange, stood in front of the courthouse with his radio-recording gear, swung it around and walked up to the first person he saw who confirmed the story on the spot and provided further evidence.

Gurjar had to push his luck out of necessity. To compete with other local journalists who were interested in covering disaster relief during one of the biggest floods in Kolhapur, he got on his motorbike in the pouring rain, drove 60km in pursuit of a rescue team and took risky photographs no one else dared to attempt.

He deliberately put himself in danger. That's not something I condone but sometimes that kind of commitment might be required for the scoop, especially in disaster relief coverage. Gurjar's antics amount to that. Not everybody is as gutsy or courageous.

COURAGE

Calculated courage may support your coverage while keeping you out of harm's way.

Zaragovia made a trip to a remote village to find coca farmers who were persuaded to make the switch to cacao. As a reporter telling the inspirational story of one man's fight to wean farmers off their coca-farming dependence, her instinct was to avoid more danger. She decided against going deeper into these remote areas where there was no cellphone coverage as she already had enough to tell the story. She had access to local knowledge and people, spoke the language and could verify her interviewees' claims in other ways.

Local knowledge and cultural understanding are often critical. In Alikaj's case, being able to relate to the people set the tone for his investigation into illegal logging. His father connected him to the driver that took him into the mountains so he could see for himself the illegal activities taking place. He had to go undercover and blend in.

Without his father's contact it would never have happened. As Alikaj told me, bonds exist between elders in Albania, in a generation that was raised under communist rule. These bonds of brotherhood run deep. That kind of trust can't be developed overnight; you need years of trust to unlock these communities. If you're not local, you won't get the access you need for the scoop.

Maybe your situation pressures you to think outside of the box. Slip a note under a door? Jump on a motorcycle to reach the key witness? Whatever the story, you'll do your best to get that knock-out source in front of your mic, on the phone or across from you.

Sourcing your scoops comes down to getting up and out and being curious. Identifying sources in the communities you want to serve— local or not—will inevitably take time. Sometimes a portion of luck or guts is required. Even if you are sitting behind a desk, the scoop will come from people in action and you'll need to collaborate across borders the bigger and more complex the story gets.

What makes a great scoop?

How many times have you picked up a headline, read the first paragraph and thought, *Why was this story written? I got it in the headline!*

We talked about how to get a scoop. Now, I'm going to zoom out and look at the composite parts of a scoop and the signals you can pick up on to recognize some journalistic rigor. The idea is, you see some or all of these parts and you can at least trust that the journalist has done their homework. These are tell-tale signs of what makes a stand-out story. Though not every story will have them, when they are present, they show journalism with a considered approach. They show some care.

Of course opinions will vary as to what a good story looks like, especially when it comes to the written word. Our tastes vary, just as the audiences we serve. Language is adaptive. Style, substance and approach will differ from publication to publication.

But generally a good story—likely written by a journalist in a newsroom which has ethical publishing guidelines—will have a few important components in the piece that demonstrate the writer's legwork beyond mere research online.

Most larger, reputable news organizations have long and detailed guidelines for journalists to follow. Some of this is the legalese of its day (any journalism school will have libel and defamation courses with good reason) and it varies from country to country. Some of it is compliance-related. Most global news organizations operating in a democratic environment will adhere to some of these principles, and some go beyond.

PEDIL

I said this book was not about writing, but there is one craft element that generally makes for a good scoop and that's the journalist's transparent revelation of the intention behind the story.

In Jack Hart's *Storycraft* on how to spin great yarn (a word Hart likes to use), I like the way he boils a good piece of writing down to the purpose it serves. I turned his guidance into a useful mnemonic: "What are you PEDIL'ing?" As in, what is the story's intention?

P = Perspective
The reader is going to get a new and fresh perspective on a person, place, thing or an issue

E = Emotion
The story will harness a powerful emotion in the reader and they will feel for the characters, place or subject

D = Diversion
Our audience is looking to escape and the piece will set out to entertain them

I = Inspiration
Having read this, you will go away fired up to fix a problem or tackle a new challenge

L = Lessons of life
The meaning behind the actions, and the deeper, more revelatory message that teaches a valuable lesson and may lead to a slice of wisdom

If a story sets out to do one or at most two of these things, it's very likely to win the audience. A good journalist will be PEDIL'ing at least one if not two of these purposes.

Zaragovia's piece on the Colombian farmers is clearly inspirational. It seeks to inspire bold, entrepreneurial action on behalf of a social cause. It also provides a fresh perspective on a long-standing issue, and it's emotive because it's one person's quest to tackle the coca farming problem.

This is true with investigative pieces too: look at Bates's piece on Prince Andrew and financier Epstein. It offers a fresh perspective and is highly emotive, evoking incredulity about the Prince's complicit silence in the scandal.

Alikaj's piece on illegal logging provides perspective and is emotive in its delivery as the readers will begin to understand the damage being done to ancient and protected forests.

The journalists don't spell out their intentions. These intentions are like little sticky corners that keep pictures in place in a photo album. Their intention frames the story to keep the reader engaged.

From the outset of each of these pieces, it's clear to the reader that the piece will offer a perspective, emotion, diversion, inspiration or life lesson. Observe your own reactions to these pieces as the journalists guide you through. Good pieces leave you feeling like you got what you came for.

Intention is not always perceptible, but when clear it will shine through. There are also more obvious markers of a great scoop.

BALANCE

Journalists can be balanced in how they approach the subjects they are reporting on. Balance is not objectivity; it's a form of transparency. What does balance mean in the context of a story anyway?

In Zaragovia's story about the cacao farmers in Colombia, we don't always see the time and effort that went into speaking to the subjects most affected by the issue. The story is about the entrepreneur Joel Palacios and what he's doing to help coca farmers. The message is positive, if anything—but it's natural to be skeptical when someone tells you of their great deeds. Should we just take Palacios' word for it?

Do these farmers even want to be helped? Balance would mean we have their view. Zaragovia certainly felt it needed to be shown, which she did with this line:

"That's left farmers like Francisco Ramírez feeling forgotten by the Colombian government. Until recently, Ramírez lived off of his 7 acres of coca."

Zaragovia wanted to provide the affected farmers the opportunity to support or dispute the entrepreneur's actions, and that's why she asked this farmer about his experience switching from coca to cacao. He served as part of the balancing act.

There are limits on the truth of anyone's testimony. The farmer in question didn't switch because he was inspired by Palacios; he was motivated by fear of FARC (Revolutionary Armed Forces of Colombia) guerrilla groups if he continued planting coca.

Zaragovia acknowledged the limits of this one source to stand up that idea in the story but, understandably, current coca farmers did not want to talk about farming the crop. Having them talk on the record might have put them and Zaragovia in danger. It was unnecessary in this case, anyway, because Palacios's assertions checked out on the ground, and Zaragovia had no reason to doubt his objectives or distrust him. Palacios staked his own reputation by speaking to Zaragovia—as Zaragovia did her own reputation by writing the story—and this personal risk signals credibility.

Zaragovia managed to get a few other voices for her story. In some cases, access was denied, blocked or otherwise impeded due to time constraints, but missing these perspectives doesn't lessen the story's transformative power.

If Zaragovia's story had been a deep investigation into government or corporate corruption, she would have needed to consider that actors might not respond and balance would be hard to achieve. In the absence of access to key actors or witnesses, what's left is a "right of reply" and we should find evidence of that in the story.

RIGHT OF REPLY

"Right of reply" means you have the opportunity to make a public comment defending yourself in response to public criticism. Simply speaking: Did all parties in the story get a chance to comment on the allegations at hand? Depending on where a newspaper is located, "right of reply" may have no legal meaning or enforcement, but it is a journalistic custom, a good strategy in any long-term relationship, and it helps to achieve the appearance of balance.

In Alikaj's story about illegal logging, where companies did not obtain required permits to carry out work, he needed evidence that he tried his best to get both the companies and the government to respond to what he found out.

He had environmental groups talking about the importance of the forest, colorfully highlighting the disastrous effect of these illegal activities, but he couldn't let their agenda dominate the story. The government and companies needed to be offered space to address these serious allegations.

Indeed, he wrote: "The environment ministry did not respond to interview requests or written questions about illegal logging."

What a let down—but at least we know he made that preliminary effort. Nor did he stop there. Alikaj went further to provide balance by getting Enver Shkurti, the director of the Environmental Inspectorate in Elbasan County, the body responsible for law enforcement in the park, to talk.

"'It is not true that there is illegal logging in the park,' said Shkurti, who was Deputy Mayor of Librazhd between 2015 and early 2018. 'Our institution does not have information about any illegal logging in the park, though there may be isolated cases.'

BIRN's investigation revealed a different picture."

This section is crucial as Alikaj has given voice to the other side. What city administrators say and stand for is in stark contrast to the evidence found on the ground. Alikaj's attempt at getting the highest power to respond—in this case the ministry responsible for permits—was absolutely necessary.

All good stories will include some form of comment, even if that means a "declined to comment" which happens when parties acknowledge that saying something could be more damaging than helpful to their reputation. Spot the denials, spot the "declined to comment" and you know that the journalist at least made an effort toward balance.

Offering the right of reply to someone who doesn't want to talk or who intends to mislead us is also one of the most frustrating aspects of a journalist's job. Inadequate responses limit our power to report and diminish the clear and transparent picture we try to provide. The story is diminished because we can't deliver a full picture. But, to those who can interpret the story, often it's also a sign that we've done something right, and a "declined to comment" hangs like someone else's guilty confession.

In Wallace's reporting about debt collection in LaGrange, no public authorities came forward to answer what he had uncovered. Public bodies and figures in a democracy should have a duty to answer questions that affect its citizens. Politicians should—at least on ethical grounds, if not legal grounds—have to answer a journalist's call, especially if the allegation is serious, true and a matter of public interest. Alas, they don't.

"There was not enough public pressure on them [local politicians]," Wallace told me. The black and immigrant electorate was oppressed by these policies and politically disengaged, he added. "I do believe, if there was more sort of democratic political pressure locally that journalism would yield different results," Wallace said.

In the end Wallace reprinted the statement supplied by the city's attorney, which in fairly weak terms defended the city's collateral debt policy as "one of many methods used to protect the financial stability of the city."

The asymmetric power of politicians over disenfranchised populations has called into question the need and validity of a right of reply. Is it our duty as good reporters to include these statements? If we know the response will be weak, indefensible and a veiled expression of innocence then why should we bother?

I'm still a staunch believer that all sides need to be heard. If the facts are stacked in a particular way, including the fact of a guilty person's denial, they can help strengthen the story and point the reader in the right direction.

In some cases, unfortunately, a right of reply gives undue voice to someone who deeply misunderstands or misrepresents the facts or effectively throws a "red herring" (a detail that misleads readers). The attorney's response to Wallace's story is a little bit like that.

Rusbridger argues in *Breaking News* that, in covering climate change, giving voice to so-called skeptics (*The Guardian* calls them "climate deniers") creates a disproportionate and undue focus on individuals who don't base their opinion on scientific fact. The climate change science is conclusive, so, unless a contrary opinion has merit for the piece, you wouldn't, on principle, give voice to a spook. Would you?

Maybe not, but if an allegation is directed at a particular climate skeptic, then you would need to give them a chance to respond. (And you might want to find a way to give them a chance to clear their own name or correct the record of their own actions without also allowing them an uninterrupted platform to air unscientific information or other unsubstantiated beliefs.) The right of reply is a tricky but necessary requirement.

There's a little more to say here. In Syed's story, representatives for Colgate, Nestlé, Unilever and L'Oréal declined to comment. (So basically all major parties subject to the story, in case you were wondering.) Why does this matter?

Media organizations print "declined to comment" to minimize the risk that they will be accused of defamation, as, if journalists give someone ample time to respond to allegations and they refuse to say anything, well, that's on them, not on the journalists.

Singh faced this situation in her story about illegal mining.

"I pretty much had all the information," she said. "I just needed them to respond to the points that I was going to make." Given more time, she might have met the mining companies in person, but there was little value they would have added and it would have delayed her story, so her eventual offer of right of reply was a curt one to cover her reporting. Her reporting included the comments she chased down.

I would go further in saying that an expanded right of reply should include anyone subject to the story, no matter how ridiculous their ideas, and even if you know that person won't be reached (because they are, for example, a world leader) or can't be reached (because they're in prison, as another example).

An "unable to reach" means the person didn't answer the phone. A "declined to comment" means we've had the person or their official representative on the phone, and they communicated their choice not to talk to us further. Not only is this outreach the fair thing to do, it's also a journalist's tool to get people to talk.

We use the right of reply as a tool to pressure people into getting back to us and force an on-record statement. Quite simply, we get them on the line and tell them we're about to publish and ask them to provide a statement on the story. Sometimes we get lucky and it's amazing how many people come clean or provide some sort of guidance about what is going on.

In a majority of cases, however, the conversation ends with a "I can't confirm or deny that," which translates as "declined to comment." (Sidenote: I urge all PR people reading this to drop the can't-confirm-or-deny lingo from their vocabulary. It doesn't mean anything and nobody reprints it that way. Just say "No comment, thanks and bye.")

Sometimes, the source or person in question will say something "on background" or "off-the-record" and here's how that goes:

"You may want to check that one fact." (Okay, set the record straight then!)

"I don't think you should publish that, it's not helpful." (Why isn't it helpful?)

"If you publish that we will sue you." (So, you're saying the story is false? What's not right about it? Tell me, because, if the story is true, I don't have anything to worry about.)

"You don't have everything quite right but here's our side of things, please don't quote me." (Wow, thanks, you just strengthened and provided the story with the necessary perspective, context and validation.)

I should note that you have to respect the person's desire not to be quoted if you care about maintaining that relationship. You should give all parties a chance to comment or air their grievances, even if you have to keep them anonymous. You never know what information might turn up.

While intention, balance and the right of reply are all part of good practice, you can also look to a story's composition for clues of great journalism and scoops worthy of your time.

LEADS

"A good lead embodies much of what the story is about—its tone, its focus, its mood. Once I sense that this is a great lead I can really start writing. It is heuristic: a great lead really leads you toward something."
—Ron Rosenbaum, *The New New Journalism*

The journalist should show you exactly where all the information is coming from in a condensed and transparent way. All quotes will be attributed, source material will be linked and ideas that come from other parties or people will be exposed. Journalists need to strike a balance, especially here.

Each morsel of information essentially comes with a caveat and needs to be checked and verified, at times painfully.

Suppose we need to state a fact in the story, like, the Empire State Building is 443 meters tall, including its antenna. A serious fact-checker might ask you to find two independent sources to confirm this is true, or else drop the mention of the building's height altogether (assuming it doesn't reveal or add anything to the story), but, realistically, we want to mention the building's height and we're not going to go out and fact-check it. We may even cut 'the antenna' qualifier from the text, because it can be assumed and because no one cares. Right? I'll let you decide.

So even facts are the basis of contention and discussion. But that is exactly the point. Facts as simple as the height of the Empire State

Building need to be discussed, just as the content of the scoop needs to be discussed.

The start of any story is hard. The reporting should guide the decision on what to lead with and sometimes a good editor leads the journalists towards the twists and turns they need to make. The lead is also a window into the sometimes gut-wrenching decisions journalists need to make, revealing both bias and sensitivity towards a particular angle, character or idea.

Alikaj's lead gambit is a dramatic scene, putting the reader into the passenger seat of a logging truck with a driver who nearly careens off the precipice of a cliff. It would be just another day for a truck driver if it weren't for the illegal activities he was engaged in.

To Alikaj the driver was just "a little fish in all of this injustice," as he put it. He not only felt bad for him as someone trying to make a modest salary to feed his family, he felt the man was honest. The driver was a victim in a million-dollar industry: running around for his bosses, carrying two phones, forging fake permits and lying to the police.

The entry point offers some tension. It also puts the reader at the heart of Alikaj's quest, which began in earnest with the trip into the forest.

The story flowed from there, as Alikaj said, and without the driver, he couldn't have amassed the evidence to put the story together. The lead is the truth as revealed through the eyes of Alikaj's reporting.

There would have been plenty of other inception points for the story. Alikaj talked to a man who was forced to cut down a tree he used to go camping under. The man had engraved the initials of his sweetheart into it. This sentimental and emotive scene could also have acted as an opener. Maybe another publication would have given this scene more prominence, but Alikaj used it to close out the story instead.

De Vrieze's point of entry is similarly emotive. It puts us right at the centre of the action with rising tension as the opener climaxes with news of a stillborn child. It also happens to be the starting point for the investigation, as it's his own stillborn child, and the one that sparked the search for answers.

In contrast to these emotive entry points, which take a few lines to develop, Bates and Syed cut straight to the chase. In fact, both of their headlines are enough to understand the premises of their stories. In Syed's scoop, the key information is at the top.

Corporate innovations and wrongdoings are often what readers are most interested in, especially those readers who use their products as consumers or have business dealings with them. At many financial newswires we talk about "actionable" leads and headlines; actionable information means that investors are able to make decisions based on the information. These leads and headlines are fact-based, true and uncompromisingly direct.

Syed wrote: "Colgate-Palmolive Co. is among bidders for the consumer arm of Nestle SA's skin-health business, people familiar with the matter said, joining an auction process that's been dominated by private equity firms."

There is an element of surprise in the lead as, up to this point, only financial buyers known as "private equity," who own a diaspora of businesses, were thought to be involved. Big companies tend to have more influence and cash than private equity, so they have a good chance at winning the bid. When they arrive at the last minute, they can frustrate the private equity firms, making their efforts costly and for naught. A lot of money is at stake.

Bates's scoop headline is very long. "Revealed: Flight logs prove Duke of York's Epstein girl WAS at key locations and on each occasion Prince Andrew was never far away—so now will he help her lawyers?" The benefit is that the reader immediately knows what this is about. Before even jumping into the lead, the article gives us all we need in bullet point form. It's a fast, direct way to get the information to the reader but you don't get context and nuance. In fact, the lead of this story provides exactly that in two very succinct sentences:

"Pressure was mounting on Prince Andrew last night to answer questions about his paedophile friend Jeffrey Epstein. Young victims of Epstein begged the Duke of York to help them get justice as the prince was offered the opportunity to give sworn testimony on 'everything he knows'."

The thing is sometimes the scoop demands immediacy and speed, and the journalist has done his job perfectly here. This is fast and furious reporting at its finest. What we don't see is the layers and layers of research that went into producing what has been distilled into just a few lines of copy.

Ross's story about sex offenders in the church lands squarely between a news story and a longer-form news feature. He had been tracking this situation for a while but there was no immediacy to the story until courts took charge. It takes on the mantle of a news story with a hook on the court's decision but fans out into a more in-depth feature about the ongoing issue.

Ross gets to the point straight away (the judge's decision) but hints at the bigger issue at stake here (the church leaders' inaction).

"After a longtime youth minister's recent conviction on corruption of minors and indecent exposure charges, a judge in this western Pennsylvania community did what the Uniontown Church of Christ's elders refused to do.

The judge told Clyde E. Brothers Jr. to stay away from church services."

Once you get to this point in the scoop, you're either going to commit (because you want the extended story) or drop it (because you have everything you need to know).

NUTS

Not all stories have this but many of the good ones do. It usually comes right after the lead. It assumes the reader's interest is already hooked, and it tells them why the story matters. It's this paragraph in Staley's piece on stroke:

"Roughly 15 million men, women, and children suffer strokes every year, and about half of them are fatal. Stroke is the second-leading killer globally, after its close cousin, heart disease, and far more deadly than cancer and the most life-threatening communicable diseases like AIDS and malaria."

This is the very reason this story matters. It provides context, and tells us what's at stake.

Zaragovia's story has a similar paragraph:

"But Palacios is swimming against the tide: Colombia's coca production has reached record numbers, according to a September report from the United Nations Office on Drugs and Crime. That's despite ongoing fumigation efforts and a program Colombia's government set up to pay farmers to voluntarily give up growing coca. The program was part of the terms of the 2016 peace treaty ending a half-century of war between Colombia's government and the Revolutionary Armed Forces of Colombia, or FARC—which controlled much of the country's cocaine business. More than 83,000 families have enrolled in the program, but the government now says funding is tight."

In newsroom language this is called a "nut graf" which gives the reader context, strengthens the lead and—in Zaragovia's story, for example—adds tension. It's the kernel or heart of the story and shows us what's at stake. It's also called the "gospel graph" in some quarters, and it's required material in Ross's story on sexual abuse in the church:

"Generations of parents entrusted Brothers with instilling Christian faith and values in their children in this city of 10,000 that originally grew with the development of coal mines and the steel industry. Victims' relatives say his case points to a problem that plagues not just the Roman Catholic Church and the Southern Baptist Convention—both embroiled in major sex abuse scandals—but also the nation's 12,000 autonomous Churches of Christ."

No starker can we see this than in Atabong's piece. He shows the suffering of one person in a war-torn environment, then fans out:

"Mbangsi can be counted among the lucky ones who have had the opportunity to give their dead ones a befitting burial or even a burial at all. Reports of abandoned corpses littered on the streets have been legion in the last two years which have seen an escalating conflict ravage

Cameroon's English-speaking region. Continuous fighting has forced many to flee, leaving behind the dead to bury the dead. Local rights organisations indicate over 1,000 civilians, armed separatists and government soldiers have been killed so far in a conflict rooted in the country's peculiar bilingual colonial history."

These are current events, and the story outlines the background material you need as a reader to understand where the journalist is headed. Even if you've never heard about the conflict in Cameroon you'll get a good sense of the problem.

Another thing about good reporting is that generally the language used is clear and uncomplicated. Style can change, and it should adapt to its audience but, generally, the reader is guided through the story effortlessly. Could you have written these paragraphs differently? Sure, but the important thing is that the nut graf exists in some form. A nut graf is an important part of that process that completes any good piece of journalism, not just a scoop.

OVER HERE

In the vein of transparency, a growing practice among journalists is the use of subtle cues to show the reader they have met with, or spoken to, the subjects in the story. All journalists I spoke to for this book do it to some degree.

Oftentimes it just isn't necessary for the journalist to announce this or make it explicit. The descriptions themselves are vivid enough for the reader to understand that Singh had been to Goa to meet residents, that Wallace had been on the ground to gather intel, and that Atabong spoke to Mbangsi. They don't need to spell it out.

Staley, by contrast, was deliberate when he wrote this into his story about the Canadian doctor, Tymianski: "Not all of NoNO's investors are wealthy, Tymianski says, and they all have his mobile number. Tymianski interrupted one of our conversations to take a call from an investor."

By providing this anecdote about Tymianski, Staley shows that he was there in the room with him, which makes the whole article a bit more readable and depicts the doctor as human. "I could have written a sentence, 'Tymianski is even known to interrupt interviews to answer...' but that would seem much more labored and artificial," Staley told me.

Putting it in this way is clearly more subjective but, as Staley noted, he inserted his own opinions to characterize him in other places too. "I spent hours with the guy, I think I can make that judgement," Staley said. We had pinpointed that he characterizes Tymianski as having a big ego, with the title of the story a nod to that idea (this one doctor believes he can take on the pharmaceutical industry where bigger and better funded companies have failed).

It's okay to insert yourself into the story but journalists should never become the story. Although, as de Vrieze's story shows, sometimes you *are* the story, embedded in ways that put your personal drive for answers at the heart of the investigation and its impact.

HEADLINES

In newsrooms, journalists call for help from "headline doctors," a chosen few who can turn weakly formulated teasers into ebullient, mysterious and enticing copy to cajole a reader to scroll beyond and get to the juicy meat of the story.

These are professionals trained to craft a headline that will stick and attract readers, especially in a metric-rich online environment which allows publications to check and recheck how well headlines and stories are doing in "real time."

The headlines for the scoops I looked at for this book didn't stand out in any unusual way. They delivered the cereal advertised on the box.

From Staley's rather lengthy "The future of stroke patients may depend on the part-time job of a Canadian surgeon" to Ross's short but musical "A Perpetrator in the Pews," these headlines evoke a sense of mystery, suspense and drama to draw their readers in.

Good headlines will do that and shout enough to engage the reader. Headlines need to be truthful, as well as crafty, subtle, playful and snappy, a way for the journalist to showcase and tease the content that is about to come. You can agonize over the headline, and you should, as it will ultimately convince readers to give your story their time.

I used to spend days agonizing over a story and its headline. In one case, a headline doctor came in and fixed it, but then once the story hit the wire I got few reads. We tend to judge our value on how many clicks a story gets, how many likes and shares it garners on social or some other metric which supposedly demonstrates our worth.

What headlines should not do is mislead, inflate, sensationalize or trivialize issues but alas, the Web is filled with precisely this kind of content. To stop this avalanche, individual action is needed and that's the subject of the final section of this book. I'm going to talk about why we need more journalists.

PART III

*A journalist's manifesto
(and why we need more journalists)*

Less news

We don't give ourselves enough credit for what we are capable of. People adapt to their situations. Each of us overcomes our own unique challenges; each time we're faced with a new challenge, we have to adapt to that, too.

What may seem insurmountable at first becomes achievable when we have to do it. We look to others for inspiration, but we can also find a similar determination in ourselves. It might not be magic after all. There might be a solution we can strategize.

So let's think about the problem of fake news. This is a serious challenge that confronts us today. Can we stop fake news? Is that an achievable goal?

Fake news travels six times faster than reputable news that contains true statements, and people are the main reason behind political falsehoods going viral, according to one MIT study. Stemming the tide of fake news in a world of instant-share and 24-hour news is hard but it can be achieved through individual action, which is great news.

Stopping fake news means the responsibility rests on our shoulders to manage the flow. And we do, in fact, have the power to stop it. That's it: Just stop it. Don't read it, don't share it. Consume no fake news or much less of it.

If only it were that easy.

Ask yourself: How many times have I caught myself sharing something to get a "like?" I glance over an article fast, don't take the time to check its validity, share it over Facebook or Twitter, and that's that. Maybe these articles didn't get much attention but sharing them still meant friends and colleagues saw them.

As regular users of social media—which includes group chats in WhatsApp—the things you and I share matter. Acknowledging that is a huge step in stopping the spread of irrelevant and fake news. Know that the buck stops with you.

Aggregation—you know, the news on your iPhone, Reddit, Facebook and other platforms that funnel traffic to your feed—is a huge problem for publishers and for journalism at large. You have willingly ceded many decisions to these internet behemoths. You've willingly given up your attention to their algorithms. If any news lands on your screen, you should question why you are seeing it in the first place.

Progress and the democratic process requires active engagement in the political system, curiosity and belief that our vote matters. If all we're doing is consuming the information we're being fed, we can be coerced and manipulated. We should judge a politician on his votes in parliament, not on the words he speaks at rallies.

I'm often fickle, too, with my news consumption. I read a headline and ten minutes later I drop something that resembles that headline into a conversation. Whether I like it or not, all that input manifests somewhere, either consciously in a "share" or in a chat, and often unconsciously in my dreams or as anxiety at bedtime.

I do my best to actively choose what to read, take the time and be deliberate. I know what it feels like to suck up every thread of information available: it leads to decision-paralysis. In turn, this leads to anxiety, insomnia, and a sense of powerlessness. Working at a newswire in the 24-hour news cycle felt like that at times. I was perpetually exhausted by all the bad news as if someone had sucked the very life out of me.

Getting clued up on everything everywhere didn't make me any smarter. On the contrary, I'd filled my mind with the useful and useless which often competed to varying degrees for the precious capital of my attention. Information over-consumption (not only news, but other types of information, too) shut me down, kept me up at night and impacted my ability to perform the next day.

Consider the thirst for information in the early days of the COVID-19 pandemic. What startled me was how much information circulated which didn't even need to be passed on. At one point, a family member shared a piece of information, acknowledging that the source was spurious. Why share it in the first place?

During the initial days and weeks of the outbreak, journalists were tracking all the official press meetings and documents that were already available from major institutional sources. The science-based information was out there but it needed to be parsed and explained. Many journalists do that as a full-time job.

If you're not employed as a journalist, you may have little time to pore through documents, but—even if you only have a few minutes!—you can "think like a journalist" and begin to vet information yourself.

You might be talking to your neighbours, your school administrators, or your company's Human Resources department to ask about travel and work-from-home. Check out what these sources are saying and don't take their word for it. Get the document that confirms your suspicions or pull up the company email. Hold these people and sources of information to account, just as a journalist would do.

If you're unhappy that the school has closed or you are panicked, the news won't help you manage your emotions. Take a break from news sources that are causing anxiety. While you're pausing your news consumption, if you need to know something, try researching it yourself offline. Go outside to check the weather. The news says it's raining over Berlin but I look out the window and there's not a drop in the sky. Call a friend who lives far away to ask about the weather in their city. Gather your own information.

In early 2020, at the beginning of the coronavirus pandemic, some people became anxious when they heard about the long list of events that had been cancelled as a health precaution. It wasn't necessary for them to follow this news. The people who are affected by specific event cancellations will know about the status of those events.

Otherwise, I don't need to know (nor do I care particularly) about whether this or that event has been cancelled. Is it helpful to me? Especially if the event is unrelated to my work and several hundred miles away? If I had a ticket to that event, I'd find out and deal with it. Right? Unless it has relevance to me, I have learned very little and it has not informed my decision-making.

Make some calls, consult with your neighbors, read local government sources, talk to your doctor, see what advice they are giving—but don't leave the news on 24 hours and bite your fingernails in fear. Quit doomscrolling the Internet if anxiety rises and you're not getting actionable information.

The news will pull you in all directions. It will take you from San Francisco to Melbourne via Beirut and leave you anxious and worried about things that are outside of your sphere of influence. When you overconsume information that isn't relevant to you, you make yourself prone to spreading disinformation.

By looking through the window of social media, where everything appears exceptional, sensational and current, you get a warped reality that often doesn't match what you are experiencing on the ground.

Sharing your own personal observations, thoughts and experiences is great. They are yours to share, but consider the source of anything else you pass on. When news and information comes from outside the margins of your world and experience, you need to assess it. We have created a lax online culture for fact-checking as not everybody upholds journalistic standards. A good rule: "when in doubt, leave it out."

Do I trust an institution such as *The New York Times* or *The Guardian* more than I trust *The Daily Wire* or *Fox News*? If I were American with skin in the game (i.e. the ability to vote people in and out of power) I might choose something like *The New York Times*—not entirely out of partisanship or my own liberal bias, but also on journalistic principles and ethics. Of course, there is a liberal bias and, yes, I might also read *Breitbart* or some other blog's take on a subject being aware that I'm reading opinion (there's space for both left and right) rather than reporting (there's really no space for "fake news"). *The New York Times* tends to tick many of the boxes discussed in this book about what constitutes a good scoop, and (unlike *Breitbart*) it also has high standards for accuracy.

Outlets have a political bias, measured and audited by organizations such as www.mediabiasfactcheck.com, which is different from the question of whether they produce factual and accurate reporting. Fake news or factually incorrect reports will show up on sites like www.snopes.com, which fact-checks individual stories for accuracy (and inaccuracies, for that matter).

In speaking to Bates, a serious hard-nosed reporter for the *Daily Mail*, I learned that tabloids have the ability to produce stories that keep the pressure up on public figures, a key function of scoop-worthy journalism. This pressure is needed if, for example, the unelected officials, such as royals, are using taxpayer money for despicable ends. With British taxpayers' money at stake, the tax-paying public has a right to know.

Do I, or should I, care about this story as a German taxpayer? Unless I'm keenly interested in royals, probably not. A well-researched article may show how the justice system has failed and with that outrage may lead you to take citizen action, or it may simply inform your vote. Bates's story does that for the people it speaks to, but it's not relevant to me. I may learn something new about the UK, but it won't inform my voting where I live.

It's a cruel reality that individuals with huge followings on social media have asymmetric power to influence and spread fake news. It's not just highly partisan and authoritarian politicians but also regular folk with thousands of followers who post misinformation, express outrage, don't understand the context and then influence like-minded people to pick up pitchforks for a cause based on fabrications.

A lot of good journalism is still free, but recognizing the good journalism from the bad journalism is tricky and we don't always have time to make a full assessment of whether the scoop is worth our time. You should always start with the basic question: "Why am I going to read this?" If you're in it for general interest (sports, or otherwise), that's fine, but the bar for a scoop is higher. Without going through everything discussed in the previous chapters to spot a good story, there's a shortcut to figuring out whether to read a piece of news, and it needs to tick these additional two boxes:

☑ I will learn something new

☑ It will help me make a better decision

After looking at the headline, consider asking these questions: "Will I learn something new here?" and "Will this piece of news help me make a more informed decision?" Doing this will eliminate a lot of junk and prevent you from reaching the point at which news consumption causes anxiety.

This isn't my idea—it's Rolf Dobelli's—but, having put these questions to the test in my own life, I believe this method is the fastest way to cut out a lot of superfluous news and reduce over-consumption. It's the simplest way to keep the news at bay and to discover relevancy. Better still, just think and act like a journalist and the right news will come to you.

THINK AND ACT LIKE A JOURNALIST

Today, you might spend an hour looking at your social media feed. *Look at that beautiful new baby boy! Wow, John's doing well for himself, looks like he's in Antigua! Politicians are corrupt! Violence is on the rise!* Joy, jealousy and facts, all packaged in 30 seconds. Now add fear, anxiety and hope in the next 30 seconds, and rinse and repeat day-in and day-out for several hours.

We haven't been wired to deal with this much emotionally charged content consistently. It's like nicotine: the sensation of the poison is exhilarating at first until you're chain smoking twenty packs a day and are unable to quit.

Each microshock of emotion depletes us of the very emotional stores that give us our ability to think and act clearly. Making more good than bad decisions will lead to a better life. Our media consumption is turning us into passive, complicit, and apathetic consumers. Some of us are entirely politically disengaged. Others have passionate political opinions, yet we spend more time reacting and venting on social media than actually engaging in politics in the real world, so we have effectively disengaged without realizing it.

What advertising did for mass consumption in the 19th century, social media is doing for mass hypnosis in this century. As Nesrine Malik brilliantly observes in *The Correspondent*: "American democracy isn't dead, it's in a coma. A deep, worrying slumber," she writes. "A certain level of fatigue sets in. The media landscape has fragmented so much that consumers can filter their information diet to those outlets that reflect their worldview," she goes on to say.

The confirmation bias has its teeth in us like a pit bull's lock jaw. Just as you get a pitbull to release by shifting its centre of gravity, you too can break the hold that your biases have on you by reevaluating your perspectives even if it initially feels painful or confusing to do so.

Thinking and acting like a journalist means starting to view your own media consumption critically. You become aware of the confirmation bias. You prioritize what matters most to you in your life. You take responsibility for what you consume, ask why you consume it and challenge its origin, purpose and purposefulness to you.

This requires effort, self-awareness and constant vigilance.

I'm not against social media and believe in its power to unite and connect. The Arab Spring, for example, is a modern democratic movement that wouldn't have been possible without Twitter. Yet that same platform gives voice to autocrats, marketeers and attention-seekers. A commitment to freedom of expression has come at the expense of enabling and amplifying abusive racists and hateful speech.

Freedom of speech doesn't necessarily involve accepting hate speech. "Freedom of speech," as it's understood differently in different countries, doesn't always mean that all speech is entirely unregulated. A person could use their freedom of speech to express their rejection of hate speech. The way the early days of social media have played out—in part due to a lack of responsibility on the part of the social media execs—hate speech has been enabled and amplified (even when not "accepted").

The problem is not the platform, it's how we use it. Just as journalists will use social media to crowdsourced journalism, we need to infuse its use with purpose. Thinking and acting like a journalist in the way you approach your news and information consumption will turn you from a lemming into a better activist for your cause.

Journalists eliminate potential sources that have shown to be untrustworthy. Thinking and acting like a journalist means selecting and curating what information you access and being brutally honest about whether it is harmful, hurtful or even fake.

Just as the journalist has intention with the piece he writes, you too have intention with what you read and share. Share a news article with intention. Tell your followers why they should care, just as a good scoop has a nut graf, which puts the entire story into context for the uninitiated.

We rely on Google, Facebook and others to present the most relevant information to us, but those algorithms do not check the reputation of news sources. The platforms aren't built to discriminate source quality. They are simply linking to news that is generating traffic, or the algorithm is using some other more complex sorting system that's beyond our comprehension.

These platforms are relying on what they know about you and your past behaviors to feed you more of the same stuff to keep you hooked, even if that means it exploits your most extreme biases and fears. Worse still, Facebook and others have relieved you of the burden of choice, serving up material it thinks you like best and that it wants you to share.

This also means you have ceded control to their version of you. No one likes the idea of being controlled, neither by despotic regimes nor by quasi-benevolent corporations. These "powers" have parsed your life into neat little boxes that claim to know who you are and who you aspire to be. Do you want that?

At a time when news is commoditized, we need to resist the temptations of mixing the fluff, fun and entertainment with the journalism that can help you and others make better decisions. Sorting through the information avalanche once fell to the newspapers. Outside of a paid subscription to a reputable newspaper, those filters are gone, so it's up to you.

You can still choose the legacy filters such as *The New York Times* or newer outlets such as *Buzzfeed* but, ultimately, this new order places far more weight on what you and your friends share and is curated by the invisible and complex algorithms of tech giants including Facebook (et al, like Instagram), Google and Twitter.

Don't get me wrong, I love Google and its news aggregation tools and the power I have when I can pull together information from all over the web in one place. I love these tools because I'm actively engaging with them, just as other journalists actively engage with the information that is strewn their way.

Because so much information is widely available online, part of the burden of sorting through and checking information has shifted away from the news and editorial teams at newspapers and now falls to you, the news consumer. You are a consumer and the news is being sold to you—no longer just by newspaper editors, but now also by tech giants. When you're a consumer, you are also not in control. You don't control the product (especially when it's free to you because advertisers are paying for you to have it). In fact, you're the product and the advertiser is in control.

You can only control what you choose to take in. The simple awareness that you are not in control of your choices means you need to think and act like a journalist and perform the key functions of sorting, keeping, discarding and deciding which information is important to you.

Thinking and acting like a journalist means you ask: Why is this information being presented to me? Did it come from a friend, a reliable news source, an aggregation platform, a Facebook ad targeting me? Or did I perform the search with specific goals and assumptions? Should I even care?

Journalists want to see a better world and, to change the world, access to the right information is critical. News traveled slower at the end of the 19th century and patchy information led to incomplete knowledge. Ignorance was rampant. The beauty now is that news can travel faster but it also means there is far too much of it for any one mind to manage.

Journalists play a crucial role in deciphering the information presented to us. We perform this function, and the public reads our work the next day (or within minutes if it's a *Bloomberg* headline). Now information can be shared, moved and distributed by anyone. Unfortunately, a lot of deceptive individuals and organizations act in their own interest. These aren't agents of truth; they are agents of advertising, manipulation, coercion and deceit.

Thinking and acting like a journalist is cutting out the irrelevant noise. That means cutting out media that merely confirms what you already believe. Indulging in political perspectives that validate your view of the world can make you less tolerant of other perspectives. You don't need to drown yourself in opposing views—especially if they contradict your core beliefs about what is good and right—but exposing yourself to other voices can help you gain the courage and awareness to rationalize and defend your perspective. Knowing how to participate in dialogue can help you stand up for your values and achieve your goals, whether that's fighting racism, upholding science, or anything else.

In today's hyper-connected world where information networks are dense and news can travel fast, people are indifferent to whether their reading material is factually accurate or not. Here's a story that was presented to me on Facebook the other day: "NASA Spots 'Potentially Hazardous' Asteroid Rapidly Approaching Earth—IGN."

I have an irrational fear of Earth being demolished by an asteroid. The chances are pretty slim. I've done a few web searches on the subject to find that it's probably not something worth panicking about (it's beyond my control, so why panic about it in the first place?). It's an irrational fear, but still, one headline intrigued me enough to click.

The article was grossly misleading. Yes, the asteroid is flying in our general direction, and it is traveling fast, but "thankfully, it'll likely miss us by a few million miles." So why did the publisher write a headline that aimed to panic me? It gets worse. The author of this article sponged a report from another report without actually checking the original source: NASA, the US space agency (which would have shown that it was going to miss Earth by a million miles and would not have inflated the issue).

There is an overabundance of choice that stymies our attention span. Behind this, algorithms work perfectly to hone our biases. The more I look up asteroid disasters on the Web, the more I'll find confirming evidence. We are not fighting a lack of information but indifference to its source. The source matters.

Facebook and other platforms, like Google, have co-opted many lines of communication, particularly those lines once serviced by newspapers to spread information. In this new paradigm, you and I become the distribution channels, because we can easily share news. So, it is paramount that we all try to uphold a certain level of integrity and transparency in our dealings, just as if we were all journalists.

Pause to consider the information you choose to put out into the world, as well as the information you seek. Don't just pick up suggested items in your news feed. Go out and actively look for an answer to the open question you have.

Journalists question their motivations and beliefs. *Are my actions defensible in a court of law? Can I trust this source? Am I going to spread a falsehood? Why am I sharing this? Is this really true?*

No matter how small your reach, there are always people who trust you and take whatever you say at face value. If you're a parent, think of how your kids copy your words and actions and use your arguments. Once these seeds are planted in their minds, they grow. No parent gets it right all the time, but you still make an effort, because you know that what you share with them in a conversation matters. Similarly, journalists share information with intention and care.

Journalists choose their words. We agonize over them in the text, consider them as we gather the information, and work with them to build a picture. Each word is a matter of accuracy and truth. Words matter because, without them, our connection to other human beings is lost. Our words leave open or shut the door to the world.

Thinking and acting like a journalist is keeping an open mind and maintaining a connection with others. Your words and actions support your goal to get at the truth. Journalists aspire to maintain relationships and to develop reliable sources. This demands an openness and empathy. Without empathy, there is emptiness, and a connection to our human nature is severed.

Reading a scoop and consuming daily news are two very different activities. One changes your perspective, opens your mind and adds value to your life. The other is just an event without context, a headline or footnote in a sea of irrelevance. Most news is pollution and washes up on the shore of your mind, turning white sands to an uninhabitable wasteland.

Will reading more than the headline drive you to make a better decision? Will it provide a fresh, new perspective? Will it teach you something? Journalists, and readers who think like journalists, ask questions and demand answers.

Journalists have to seek new perspectives all the time and hear all sides. With their minds on jury duty, the longer and deeper they progress into a subject, the more perspectives open up, and eventually they may find an answer.

Thinking and acting like a journalist means you claim ignorance until you've talked to enough people to form a well-balanced opinion. This might not happen overnight, but you'll know when you've begun to glimpse the big picture. Remember the Kaplan-Meier curve discussed earlier in this book, which reveals the effectiveness of a cancer drug? Most people don't need a deep scientific understanding of how the curve works; they only need to know how to read and interpret what it implies about a situation. This kind of big-picture understanding—on just about any topic!—will begin to emerge when you listen to diverse sources.

Journalists don't pretend to have the answer when we don't actually know. This is particularly difficult because others expect us to be experts. At times, we all nod in agreement to save face even if we haven't understood what is going on. Staring down our ignorance is both humbling and courageous. During the course of our investigations, journalists are routinely faced with this dilemma.

As journalists, we don't claim to know everything, but we need to learn enough to transpose and decode the different languages people speak. We partake in the learning of new perspectives from the experts we speak to.

Thinking and acting like a journalist will disrupt and improve your online presence and behaviour, improve your reputation with better and clearer communication, and help you perform your civic duties with more clarity. It will also elevate others to question their online behavior and habits.

Journalists, as individuals, broadly speaking, are working towards a better world. When journalists produce good information (accurate, relevant, and clearly communicated) and defend people's right to access it, they are creating the change they wish to see. Everyone relies on good information whether or not we consciously value it. When we are well informed, we are better able to uphold and pursue our own values, whatever those may be.

Journalism is a public service even though, in high-information societies where news is taken for granted, it is rarely recognized by non-academics and non-readers for the work it does to inform, educate and empower individuals and communities.

If it's inevitable that traditional journalism will die in the noise of an information-saturated society, we need more individuals thinking and acting like journalists, with a view to providing this public service. A "public" or audience might be the 500 friends you have on Facebook. It might sound small, but this has significant power.

If we all think and act a bit more like journalists in the way we create and share our experiences, it will be easier to stem the tide of fake news, strengthen our democratic institutions, and steer us all towards a more equitable world and planet worth inhabiting.

Journalism is an ethos that places us at the forefront of upholding our truths and requiring us to always think before we share. We need less news and more people acting like journalists. When this happens, there will be a greater demand for scoops that matter, and we will find the resources to defend and produce them.

Epilogue

"Seeing something that the government claims is good and pointing out why it is bad is an essential function of journalism." —*The Economist*

Behind the Scoop: Why you should think and act like a journalist grew out of my own fear that journalism is a dying art. It's not; it's just under some heavy artillery fire. I'm not ready to concede it's dying.

The neat power structures in which the press acted as a gatekeeper and directed the flow of information have been effectively dismantled. That's not a bad thing. It just means new power structures and centres are emerging, and individuals are once again at the centre of this fight.

In Evelyn Waugh's *Scoop*, a satirical take in 1938 on the news industry of its day, journalists had real power. One such correspondent "cabled off a thousand word story about barricades in the streets, flaming churches [...] in less than a week there was an honest to God revolution under way."

The big newspapers satirically described by Waugh have been challenged and their power dispersed across the very expanse of the Internet. Finding journalism's place in this expanse is the challenge of our time.

Of course there is new, hard-hitting, data-driven, digital-savvy journalism. Will it have readers? I sure hope so. I worry that the type of journalism described in the pages of this book might not even find its way to you because many of the gatekeeping newspapers and portals of yesteryear are gone.

Given the plethora of portals—and I'm openly biased about this—we need more journalists in the world. The more people are actively hunting for truth, the easier it will be for the most courageous and dedicated among us to unearth the biggest injustices and most shocking abuses of power.

Freedom of speech has declined globally in the last decade even as information access and its flow has swelled. This seems both counterintuitive and contrary to the grand vision of the Internet as a democratizing force. Instead, we have free-flowing information turned into a source of anarchy used by autocratic governments to legislate away the freedom of speech, to the detriment of truth-seeking journalists who are forced to toe the line.

In Ethiopia, one of 25 governments to shut down the Internet in 2018, people were desperate for information following an attempted coup. India has tightened its stranglehold on Kashmir with internet censorship. Freedom of expression, whether that translates into freedom of the press or the right to speak out against power, is a cornerstone of a democracy.

We each possess the power to publish anything at any time—including that which is factually untrue—but we are still somewhat blind to our own power. In the age of the personal publishing revolution, we can tell truths and dispel falsehoods but also tell lies and spread falsehoods. The news dies as quickly as it surfaces. The shelf-life of a Facebook post or a Tweet is mere seconds before it is drowned out in the cacophony of clicks.

Traditional journalism has always been about providing people the ability to make decisions. If what we produce helps people make better decisions, then it has fulfilled at least part of its function in a democracy.

The information news outlets disseminate must give purpose to thousands of decision-makers everyday, from the shopkeeper to CEOs.

This journalism is not "news"; it is context, understanding and perspective. Sometimes it speaks to an audience of one, but that's one more mind opened to the possibility of a truth uncovered.

As Freedom House, an independent watchdog, points out, even in democracies that champion free speech, leadership has "made explicit attempts to silence critical media voices and strengthen outlets that serve up favorable coverage."

According to the watchdog, media freedom has been deteriorating around the world over the past decade, with new forms of repression taking hold, including but not limited to authoritarian governments. Social media has also been co-opted as a tool for repression, election rigging and the targeted spread of misinformation.

Facebook is under fire as a cesspool of targeted fake news ads with which Russia interfered in the 2016 US presidential election. We need only to think of Donald Trump's repeated Twitter attacks on the media and journalists.

I've had my own run-in with a democratic government under which speech is only quasi-free during a short stint in Honduras in the early 2000s. I was given press credentials to cover a high-level meeting of delegates who were discussing a regional trade deal. I received a personal letter from the then-President's office, ordering me to respect only official statements or—not quite in these words—face the consequences. I was essentially muzzled. What was I to do?

The local paper I was writing for feared government retribution and a coverage blackout, so the demonstrations taking place in front of the hotel ended up a footnote in the story. Journalists face these threats everywhere, and, "in the last few years, 130 journalists have been killed, 300 have been imprisoned for their work," according to Chatham House.

It's not just about freedom of speech; it's about getting the right information to the right people at the right time. The work of journalists could, for example, encourage people to stay away from places where high levels of a virus are being reported during a global pandemic. This is important for the citizens of countries run by autocrats as well as for foreigners living under that regime—because the autocrats themselves are unlikely to release these kinds of facts—and it supports a truly global response to a global problem.

China's handling of the COVID-19 crisis in its early days of December 2019 was a reminder that those with first-hand information on the potential impact of the virus—those with "an ear to the ground"—needed to be heard. Doctors in China who communicated their findings about the virus acted as good journalists. Sadly, they were silenced initially.

Facts about the spread of the virus need to be checked, verified and contested without unnecessary delay. The public needs access to that information to protect their health. Citizen journalists (if that's what these Chinese doctors might be called) have a strong role to play as governments aren't trustworthy. It falls on journalists to report out these new findings.

To revive journalism's value in today's world, we should celebrate the highest forms of journalism and steer our focus towards a more equitable, fair, transparent and functional democracy.

This isn't easy, as journalism is a messy affair. If the previous chapters are anything to go by, you'll see that individual bias can be both a strength and a weakness, and that writing stories involves human judgement and fallacy.

The news business has always had a "recency bias," what we now tend to call the "24-hour news cycle." A *Washington Post* political reporter, the late David Broder, saw newspapers and the journalism contained in them as "partial, hasty, incomplete, inevitably somewhat flawed and inaccurate rendering of the things we heard about in the last 24 hours." It's a statement Rusbridger returns to multiple times in his book *Breaking News*.

This has deep echoes of Dobelli's view of journalists in his essay "Avoid News" in which many journalists just "cobble together the rest of the news from other people's reports, common knowledge, shallow thinking and whatever the journalist can find on the Internet." Less than 10% of news is original, he posits, and only 1% is investigative.

Not all journalists aspire to do investigative work. As exemplified by some of the journalists in this book, there are plenty of important and impactful original scoops that might not qualify as "investigative" in Dobelli's judgement.

My definition of a scoop is broader and more inclusive. It seeks to inspire more people to consider their investigations as scoop-worthy: if not revelatory in the sense of Watergate, then still important to those with an interest and stake in unlocking their understanding of the world.

These individual contributions aren't worth less just because they didn't break the news. Individuals doing their job with an ear to the ground should believe that their perspective matters a great deal, even when the story is ongoing, just like the perspective of those Chinese doctors in the early days of the COVID-19 pandemic.

We all have power. Many of us just haven't discovered or harnessed it yet.

BONUS

The 12 monkeys

How and why did I end up with twelve journalists and these stories? Let's call it the divine, mythical inclinations of ancient Greece, a dodekatheon. I could have called them 12 Olympians but leaned towards the more dystopian film "12 Monkeys" starring Brad Pitt.

Misplaced allegories aside, I was looking for a broad selection of stories and journalists. Half came via the Hostwire platform. (If you're a journalist, please get on there. It's a great place to meet and collaborate with other journalists around the world.) The other half are from my network or I specifically reached out to them as I saw something online that piqued my interest.

Ross was embroiled in a situation where one of his scoops was appropriated by a national outlet and he was never credited, so I thought he'd be fun to talk to. He also covered an area I knew very little about: religion.

Wallace rose to prominence for a short amount of time writing about how he was fired for being too outspoken (I'll leave it at that for now). He subsequently wrote a book which fit into my research (*The View from Somewhere: Undoing the Myth of Journalistic Objectivity*). He is a high-calibre journalist criticizing the role of journalism in history; outspoken, having also been quoted in *The New York Times* as an expert on the subject; and transgender, a minority among journalists.

Sarah Syed and Oliver Staley are former *Bloomberg* colleagues and I've always appreciated their views, approaches and perspectives. So I felt naturally inclined to include them. Daniel Bates reached out to me on a whim and I decided to humor him, even though I felt I had already completed my research. I'm glad I did because he provided a new and fresh perspective that I hadn't yet considered.

I could have gone for household names on the Pulitzer Prize list but that was not really the point. I fed some of those views in, anyway, through my reading. Had I pursued interviews with those people, I would have spent more time trying to get access to the top brass than actually learning something. Besides, I'm championing journalists and voices you might not ordinarily see in a book like this. That's a key reason for journalism in the first place—to shine a light on some of those characters who have been working tirelessly behind the scenes and don't always get the recognition they deserve. I enjoy flying the flag for journalists who, in their own right, deserve recognition for what they do (even if they don't seek it).

Going back over the list of journalists, you'll see we've covered everything from politics, business, culture and the environment, published across multiple platforms, though admittedly the general focus was on the written scoops. They come from various online, local, and national broadsheets covering a variety of investigative topics: corruption at a national level, highly secretive business dealings, uncovering gross social inequalities and exposing the impact of climate change and a warped healthcare system. They are men (including a transgender man) and women and they are from Germany, India, Albania, the Netherlands, the USA, the UK and Cameroon.

Though I tapped my own network, as well as platforms like Hostwire (built in my hometown, Berlin), the 12 journalists in this book came largely to me. I had no script for meeting any kind of gender-specific quota or covering all geographies, or hitting a set number of interviews before deciding enough was enough. I did things the way I like to approach things and that's organically. Unfortunately I also had to turn down a few requests as they didn't fit my criteria.

What criteria, you might ask? I wanted to look at standout investigative pieces: covering corruption, uncovering wrong-doing, or illuminating injustices be they social or environmental issues. The thirst for investigating something that seems "off" or "wrong" is at the heart of journalism and is also the mark of a great story, whether it wins prizes or not.

Furthermore, I sought original reporting. Original reporting meant the journalist went out and talked to a real person. They didn't just do desk research. They were out there getting something: a document, a quote or an angle nobody else had.

That sort of hard-nosed reporting, which requires you to get off your seat and sit down with someone face-to-face, is a dying art but it is exactly this journalism we need in today's use-and-discard day and age. We need the journalism that takes time and sheds light on something new and sometimes scandalous. It exposes rampant power, or sticks up for those parts of society that are being oppressed by this power. It reveals injustice, but it doesn't merely shed light on the problem—it also starts to point toward a solution. It shows how to overcome obstacles. It inspires.

The interviews that came together surprised me largely because I didn't really know what to expect, nor was I confident of finding the right candidates. I went into the process without any expectation and came out with 12 interviews and incredible stories. No one declined my request for an interview and the response was overwhelming. I'm grateful for their participation.

I thought I was done with journalism. I was ready to kick this profession but felt called to write this book. As the project evolved, and as a two-month research window became four months, I learned from it. Journalism is not dead; it can thrive in us, if we open up to its possibilities.

Join The Journalist Community

Now you know how some of the best journalists in the world research, write and get their scoops published. Maybe you're looking to enter the profession or write a scoop?

From getting the idea, and following it through to writing and pitching, you'll need help to develop your own process to reproduce story, after story, after story, after story.

Being a journalist is hard. Making ends meet is hard, too, but you're dedicated, right? Nobody can do anything alone, which is why I've built a community with over 400 journalists to help you get better at what you do and a place for you to get help.

No matter what publication you are shooting for, if you just want help getting started or on-the-job advice, then start building your portfolio, reputation and credibility and get The Journalist Community to help.

Here's what *The New York Times* says today about its journalism: "Either you cover the world or you don't. There are no halfway measures. Our International correspondents, who are overseen by editors in New York, Hong Kong and London and helped by an army of support staff, are given one basic marching order: If you get wind of a story, do whatever it takes to chase it and let us worry about the bills."
—Michael Slackman, International Editor

If that kind of career appeals to you, you'll have to get bylines, build your portfolio and develop a system to keep breaking, writing and producing stories with impact. The rest will flow from there.

If you need some help, accountability, and resources to help you on your way, as well as like-minded journalists with whom you can bounce ideas back and forth, then join The Journalist Community, a private group for journalists who want to get ahead, get help and share in their success.

JOIN NOW
facebook.com/groups/202411423982180

Enter "THESCOOPBOOK" in the questions box on how you heard about the group and you'll get a fast-track entry. What are you waiting for?

—Johannes

ACKNOWLEDGEMENTS

This book would not have been possible without Meg, my wife, who has been so patient with me as I went through the ups and downs of putting this together.

A huge hug for my very close friend and confidant Adrien Raphoz who designed the cover and did all the graphics and without whom this book would look a shambles. If you need someone who knows what they are doing, book him (pun not intended).
creativeparty.carbonmade.com

A big thanks goes out to Tucker Lieberman, who answered my cry for help on Twitter and ripped through this text beautifully as my editor and Rachael Cox, who typesets quickly and efficiently. My beta readers, Tom Hayton, Renzo D'Andrea, Mike Cunnington, Frédéric Dubois, Nuala Gallagher, Dan Spacie and Nicolas Bereni swept through this book and provided important feedback for essential improvements.

I've thanked my interviewees but they are central to this book and supported me throughout, so Bobby Ross Jr., Jop de Vrieze, Sarah Syed, Anna Codrea-Rado, Amindeh Blaise Atabong, Oliver Staley, Shalini Singh, Abhijeet Gurjar, Arlis Alikaj, Lewis Wallace, Veronica Zaragovia and Daniel Bates, you rock.

I'd also like to thank you, the reader, for pouring over these pages and spending your precious time with me. Thank you.

URGENT PLEA!

Thanks for reading my book.

I really appreciate all the feedback and need to hear
what you have to say.

The most successful people thrive on feedback and I want to make
this and future books better and improve my work.

Please leave a helpful review on Amazon letting me know what you
think of the book.

Thank you!

Johannes

Printed in Great Britain
by Amazon